# Colman's Book of
# TRADITIONAL BRITISH COOKERY

J. Audrey Ellison

Fielde Mustarde

Colman's Book of

# TRADITIONAL BRITISH COOKERY

J. Audrey Ellison

Ward Lock Limited · London

The author and publisher would like to acknowledge the help of Counsel Limited in the preparation of this book.

Photography: Barry Bullough: front jacket, back jacket, 17, 35, 45, 47, 57, 76. Alan Duns: 18, 36, 46, 48, 101, 103, 104. Paul Kemp: 102. Anthony Kay: 58. Vic Paris: 75.

Woodcuts from *The Herball or Generall Historie of Plantes* by John Gerarde (1597), courtesy of the Trustees of the British Museum (Natural History).

Line drawings by Gillian Zeiner.



First published in Great Britain in 1980 by Ward Lock Limited, 116 Baker Street, London W1M 2BB, a Pentos Company.



Designed by Chris Walker.
Text filmset 10/12pt Times New Roman by Asco Trade Typesetting Ltd., Hong Kong.

Printed in Singapore by Kyodo-Shing Loong Printing Industries Pte Ltd.

# Contents

# Introduction

Mustard, in one form or another, has been known since the earliest times. It has been traced back as far as 3000 BC in India, and there are numerous Greek, biblical, medieval and Shakespearian references to the plant and its properties. In these earlier times it was widely credited with medicinal powers, and was held to be the remedy for many ailments, including snake-bites and toothache. More realistically perhaps, before methods of preserving meat had been developed, mustard was used to mask unpleasant flavours, and to aid digestion.

The Romans are reputed to have introduced mustard to Britain, and it grew to wide popularity in the Middle Ages and Tudor times. In Henry VII's reign, for example, the Earl of Northumberland allowed his tenants 160 gallons of mustard seed every year.

Mustard makers would pound the seed by hand in a mortar, until in 1720 a Mrs. Clements of Durham conceived the idea of grinding the mustard seed, and then sifting it to obtain a fine flour just like wheat-flour. She took this powder to London where 'George the First stamped it with fashion by his Approval'.

In 1742, Messrs. Keens set up a factory for mustard manufacture at Garlick Hill, London and this probably explains the phrase 'as keen as mustard' They continued making mustard until they were taken over by J. & J. Colman in 1903.

Jeremiah Colman started milling mustard in 1814 at Stoke Holy Cross, a watermill four miles south of Norwich. The business grew rapidly and in 1854

Colmans moved to a large site at Carrow on the outskirts of the city. The present mill was opened in 1959.

Colmans have continued to develop the growing and refining of the very finest mustards, and today more mustard is traded than any other spice in the world.

Garden Muftard

## Mustard in the making

Colmans contract with farmers to cultivate two distinct mustard crops—'brown' and 'white' seed. Over the years, Colmans' plant breeders have produced a succession of improved strains, culminating in the latest Newton (brown) and Kirby (white) named after the Norfolk parishes in which they were developed.

The seed is sown between mid March and the end of April. The characteristic yellow fields of flowering mustard can be seen throughout June in eastern England. Mustard is a prolific yielder and may increase as much as two thousandfold in a season.

Harvesting takes place in late August and early September, using combine harvesters. The seed is delivered in bulk to Colmans for grading, cleaning, careful drying and storage in a concrete silo of over 9000 tonnes capacity.

The two types of seed when milled both give flours of a rich yellow colour. When the flour is mixed with water, essential flavouring oils are released. In the case of brown mustard, these give a volatile, pungent flavour. White mustard also gives a sensation of heat, but this develops more rapidly and is lost sooner.

The two types of mustard seed therefore result in flavours which are complementary to one another. The flours obtained from them are blended in varying proportions, according to the product desired. As well as traditional dry mustard powder, Colmans

Wilde Mustard

manufacture and pack several varieties of prepared mustard in jars and tubes. Hot English mustard is made by blending fresh mustard flour with other pre-cooked ingredients. French, German and American mustards are milder, vinegar-based varieties which also contain herbs and spices.

Then there are Colmans' French Speciality mustards—Meaux, Dijon and Bordeaux. Meaux is pleasantly hot with a coarse texture. Dijon has a piquant flavour and is made from brown seed moistened with grape juice. The Bordeaux is a smooth mild mustard, aromatic and herbal.

## Cooking with mustard

Recipes specify either dry mustard, or prepared mustard. Where prepared mustard is called for, this may be used directly from the jar, or dry mustard may be blended with a little cold water or milk, to make a creamy paste. The fully developed flavour of home-made mustard diminishes with standing, so to obtain maximum pungency for cooking or table use, blend the powder with the liquid just 10 minutes before use.

The dishes in this book have been carefully selected to represent the finest traditional British cooking. As the only spice widely grown in this country, mustard has a long association with many of these traditional recipes. It will enhance the flavour of almost any savoury dish and, contrary to popular belief, is not a fiery spice when used in powder form in cooking.

*Notes*

It is important to follow **either** the metric **or** the Imperial measures in any one recipe.
All spoon measures are level.
Flour is plain and sugar is granulated unless specified otherwise.

# Soups

## Oxtail Soup

*6 portions*

Divide the oxtail into joints, put into a large pan of cold water and bring to the boil. Drain off the water, rinse the joints and dry them thoroughly with absorbent paper. Melt the dripping in a heavy saucepan and brown the joints quickly in the hot fat. Transfer the joints to a large saucepan. Fry the carrots, onion and celery. Add them to the oxtail with the stock, herbs, spices and lemon rind. Cover and simmer for 2 hours.

Strain off the stock and when cold skim off all the fat. Remove the meat from the oxtail and cut it into small pieces. Blend the flour with a little of the cold stock. Return the rest of the stock to the saucepan. Stir in the flour thickening and oxtail meat. Bring to the boil, stirring continuously. Simmer for 3 to 5 minutes. Add the sherry and taste for seasoning.

1 medium-sized or ½ large oxtail (1–1.5kg/2–3lb)
50g/2oz dripping
2 carrots, sliced
1 onion, sliced
1 stick celery, sliced
2.5 litres/4 pints stock
1 bay leaf
1 sprig marjoram
1 sprig thyme
2 teaspoons prepared mustard
6 peppercorns
2 cloves
1 piece lemon rind
25g/1oz flour
100ml/4fl oz sherry
salt, pepper

# Scotch Broth

*4 portions*

4 tablespoons dried split green peas
1kg/2lb neck of mutton
2 tablespoons pearl barley
1.2 litres/2 pints water
1 carrot, diced
1 onion, diced
1 turnip, diced
2 leeks, shredded
$\frac{1}{4}$ cabbage, shredded
1 tablespoon chopped parsley
salt, pepper

Soak the dried peas in cold water overnight. Drain and rinse. Cut the mutton from the bones into pieces about 5cm/2 inches square. Trim off and discard the fat. Put the meat, bones, pearl barley and water into a saucepan. Bring to the boil and skim. Add the diced vegetables, leeks, cabbage and soaked peas. Simmer very gently for about $2\frac{1}{2}$ hours. Remove the bones and skim off the fat. Add the parsley and seasoning to taste, then serve.

# Cock-a-leekie Soup

*6–8 portions*

3kg/6lb boiling chicken
2.5 litres/4 pints water
2 teaspoons salt
$\frac{1}{4}$ teaspoon pepper
1 blade mace
6 leeks, shredded
50g/2oz long-grain rice
2 tablespoons chopped parsley

Place the boiling chicken in a large saucepan with the giblets, water and seasonings. Bring to the boil slowly. Skim and simmer gently for 2 hours. Remove the chicken for serving as a main dish with parsley sauce. Remove and discard the giblets and mace.

Preferably allow the liquor to cool in order to skim off excess fat more easily. Add the leeks and rice to the broth and simmer for about 20 minutes until the rice is tender. Add a little chopped chicken breast and the parsley, and adjust the seasoning.

# Game Soup

*4–6 portions*

Melt the butter in a heavy saucepan. Add the vegetables and fry them lightly for 5 minutes. Stir in the flour and cook for 2 to 3 minutes. Add the broken up bird carcasses, then the stock and seasoning. Bring to the boil, stirring frequently. Cover the pan and simmer very gently for about 2 hours. Strain the soup and reheat with the redcurrant jelly and sherry or port. Serve with croûtons.

75g/3oz butter
2 carrots, diced
1 turnip, diced
1 onion, chopped
2 sticks celery, chopped
50g/2oz flour
2 or more carcasses of game birds
900ml/1½ pints beef stock
salt, pepper
2 teaspoons redcurrant jelly
2 tablespoons cooking sherry or port
fried croûtons

# Lentil Soup

*6 portions*

Soak the lentils in cold water overnight. Drain and rinse. Heat the butter in a saucepan. Add the onion and carrot, cover and gently sauté for about 10 minutes, shaking the pan frequently. Add lentils, stock, bouquet garni, salt and pepper. Bring to the boil, cover and simmer for 1½ hours. Remove the bouquet garni and rub the lentils through a fine sieve or purée in an electric blender.

Return the purée to a clean pan. Blend the flour with a little of the milk. Stir the rest of the milk into the purée, then stir in the flour thickening. Bring to the boil, stirring constantly, and simmer for 5 minutes. Taste for seasoning. Sprinkle each bowl with a little chopped parsley on serving.

225g/8oz split red lentils
25g/1oz butter
1 onion, sliced
1 carrot, sliced
1.2 litres/2 pints ham-bone stock
1 bouquet garni
salt, pepper
1 tablespoon flour
600ml/1 pint milk
2 tablespoons chopped parsley

# Potato Soup

*4 portions*

40g/1½oz butter
1 onion, chopped
400g/14oz potatoes, sliced
1.3 litres/2¼ pints stock
1–2 tablespoons flour
100ml/4fl oz single cream
salt, white pepper

Melt the butter in a saucepan and gently fry the onion and potatoes for 10 minutes, then add the stock. Bring to the boil and simmer until the potatoes are tender. Beat the soup vigorously to purée the potatoes. Mix together the flour and cream and blend into the soup to thicken it. Simmer for a few minutes to cook the flour. Season to taste and serve.

*Note:* If a smoother soup is required, sieve the soup before thickening and use double cream instead of single.

# Artichoke Soup

*4–6 portions*

1kg/2lb Jerusalem artichokes
lemon juice
25g/1oz butter
1 onion, sliced
1 stick celery, chopped
1.2 litres/2 pints stock
salt, black pepper
pinch ground nutmeg
300ml/½ pint milk
25g/1oz flour
1 tablespoon chopped parsley

Peel and slice the artichokes, putting them straight into water to which lemon juice has been added to prevent them from browning. Melt the butter in a heavy saucepan and add the drained artichokes, the onion and the celery. Cover and cook for a few minutes, shaking the pan occasionally to prevent the vegetables from sticking and browning. Add the stock and seasoning and simmer until the vegetables are tender. Rub through a nylon sieve or purée in an electric blender.

Reheat the purée with 200ml/6fl oz of the milk. Blend the flour with the rest of the milk and add to the soup. Bring to the boil, stirring continuously. Cook for about 5 minutes. Adjust the seasoning. Serve with a little parsley sprinkled on each bowl.

# Green Pea Soup

*4 portions*

- 600g/$1\frac{1}{4}$lb shelled peas
- 1.2 litres/2 pints chicken stock
- 1 sprig mint
- sprigs parsley
- 15g/$\frac{1}{2}$oz butter
- $1\frac{1}{2}$ tablespoons flour
- 2 tablespoons chopped parsley
- 1–2 teaspoons grated onion
- 150ml/$\frac{1}{4}$ pint single cream or top of the milk
- salt, white pepper

Cook the peas in the stock with the mint and parsley for 10 to 20 minutes until the peas are tender. Remove the mint and parsley. Strain off the stock and rub the peas through a sieve or purée them in an electric blender.

Melt the butter, stir in the flour and cook for 2 to 3 minutes, stirring well. Add the stock by degrees, bring to the boil, stirring, and simmer for 3 minutes. Stir in the pea purée and return to the boil. Add the chopped parsley, grated onion and cream or top of the milk, and adjust seasoning to taste. Serve hot or chilled.

# Lettuce Soup

*4 portions*

- 1 lettuce
- 25g/1oz butter
- 6–8 spring onions, chopped
- 2 medium-sized old potatoes, cut into pieces
- 1 litre/$1\frac{3}{4}$ pints chicken stock
- 150ml/$\frac{1}{4}$ pint single cream or top of the milk
- salt, black pepper
- 1 tablespoon finely chopped chervil
- fried croûtons (optional)

Wash the lettuce and tear up the leaves. Melt the butter and lightly fry the lettuce and spring onions in it, to soften them without browning. Add the potatoes and stock. Simmer for about 30 minutes until the potatoes are cooked. Put through a nylon sieve or vegetable mill, or purée in an electric blender. Add the cream or top of the milk. Reheat and add seasoning to taste. Sprinkle with chervil. Croûtons may be served with this soup.

# Cheese & Egg Dishes

## Cheese Pudding

*4 portions*

175g/6oz fresh breadcrumbs
salt, white pepper, cayenne pepper
100g/4oz grated cheese
2 large eggs
2 teaspoons prepared mustard
300ml/$\frac{1}{2}$ pint milk
40g/$1\frac{1}{2}$oz butter
sprigs parsley

Butter a 750ml/$1\frac{1}{4}$ pint pie dish. Season the breadcrumbs with salt and white pepper. Arrange them in the pie dish in alternate layers with the grated cheese. Beat the eggs with the mustard and add them to the milk. Pour over the crumb and cheese layers. Dot the top with butter divided into pats. Bake at 170°C/325°F/gas 3 for 45 minutes. Sprinkle lightly with cayenne pepper and garnish with parsley.

# Bacon and Cheese Tart

*4 portions*

Line a 20cm/8 inch flan tin with the pastry. Cut the bacon rashers into small squares and cook them in a dry frying pan until the fat runs. Put the grated cheese at the bottom of the flan and place the bacon pieces on top. Beat together the eggs, egg yolk, cream and mustard. Pour on to the bacon. Bake for 30 minutes at 200°C/400°F/gas 6. Serve hot or cold, with a salad.

- shortcrust pastry, using 175g/6oz flour, etc (see below)
- 100g/4oz smoked streaky bacon
- 75g/3oz grated Cheddar cheese
- 2 eggs
- 1 egg yolk
- 300ml/$\frac{1}{2}$ pint single cream or cream and milk mixed
- 1 teaspoon prepared mustard

# Shortcrust Pastry

Sift the flour and the salt. Rub the fats into the flour until the mixture resembles fine, even breadcrumbs. Add water and mix to a firm dough. Use as required.

- 225g/8oz flour
- pinch salt
- 50g/2oz butter
- 50g/2oz lard
- about 2 tablespoons cold water

# Cauliflower Cheese

*4 portions*

1 cauliflower
40g/$1\frac{1}{2}$oz butter
40g/$1\frac{1}{2}$oz flour
$\frac{1}{2}$ teaspoon salt
white pepper
400ml/$\frac{3}{4}$ pint milk
2 teaspoons prepared mustard
150g/5oz grated mature Cheddar cheese
3 tablespoons golden breadcrumbs

Rinse and trim the cauliflower, discarding any coarse leaves and tough stalk. Put the cauliflower into a saucepan of boiling salted water so that it is half-immersed in the water. Cook for 15 to 20 minutes with the lid almost covering the pan until the cauliflower is barely tender. Be careful not to overcook.

Meanwhile prepare the cheese sauce by melting the butter and stirring in the flour. Cook for 2 to 3 minutes without colouring. Add the seasonings. Remove from the heat and gradually add the milk, stirring constantly. Return to the heat and bring to the boil, still stirring. Add the mustard and 75g/3oz grated cheese. Simmer for about 3 minutes.

Drain the cooked cauliflower thoroughly and divide into florets. Place in a buttered flameproof dish. Pour over the sauce. Sprinkle with the remaining grated cheese and the breadcrumbs. Brown in a hot oven at 220°C/425°F/gas 7 for about 10 minutes. Alternatively, brown under a hot grill.

# Cheese Straws

*40 straws*

100g/4oz flour
salt, white pepper, cayenne pepper
$\frac{1}{2}$ teaspoon dry mustard
50g/2oz butter
50g/2oz grated cheese
1 egg yolk
1 tablespoon cold water

Sift the flour, salt and mustard into a basin and rub in the butter. Add the cheese and remaining seasonings. Mix to a stiff paste with the egg yolk and water and turn out on to a floured board. Roll out to about 5mm/$\frac{1}{4}$ inch thick and cut into narrow strips about 7.5cm/3 inches long and about 5mm/$\frac{1}{4}$ inch wide. Bake at 200°C/400°F/gas 6 for about 10 minutes until crisp.

# Scotch Eggs

*4 portions*

Mix together the sausagemeat, mustard, tomato ketchup, herbs and seasonings. Divide into four. Using floured hands, mould sausage mixture around each of the hard-boiled eggs, to enclose completely. Brush with beaten egg, and coat with crumbs. Repeat to double-coat the eggs. Deep fry in hot oil at 182°C/360°F for about 8 minutes, until golden brown and cooked through. Drain and cool. Serve cold with salad.

450g/1lb sausagemeat
1 tablespoon prepared mustard
$1\frac{1}{2}$ tablespoons tomato ketchup
pinch dried mixed herbs
salt, pepper
4 hard-boiled eggs
1 egg, beaten
golden breadcrumbs
oil for deep frying

# Stuffed Eggs

*3–4 portions*

Halve each egg and remove the yolks. Cut a small slice off the rounded side of each half so that they will stand upright. Sieve the yolks. Mash the sardines with the mustard, grated onion and lemon juice and then add the yolks. Blend well together and season to taste. Fill the whites with the mixture, using a piping bag if you wish. Serve the eggs on a large platter lined with shredded lettuce, garnished with tomato quarters, olives and onion rings.

6 hard-boiled eggs
125g/4oz canned sardines
1 teaspoon dry mustard
1 teaspoon grated onion
2 teaspoons lemon juice
salt, pepper
tomato quarters
olives
onion rings

*Previous page: Cock-a-leekie soup (recipe page 10).*
*Opposite: Stuffed eggs (recipe above).*

# Mumbled Eggs

*4 portions*

8 eggs
2 teaspoons prepared mustard
salt, pepper
50g/2oz finely chopped mushrooms
25g/1oz butter
50g/2oz cream cheese or soft cheese
1 tablespoon cream or top of the milk
4–8 slices toasted bread, cut into triangles

*Savoury Butter*
25g/1oz butter, softened
1 teaspoon prepared mustard
1 teaspoon finely chopped parsley

To make the savoury butter, cream the butter with the mustard and parsley.

Beat the eggs with the mustard and season with salt and pepper. Stir in the chopped mushrooms. Melt the butter in a pan over a low heat. Add the eggs and mushrooms and stir until they begin to set. Add the cheese and stir for several minutes until the cheese is thoroughly incorporated and the eggs are cooked. Stir in the cream or top of the milk and serve at once on a large dish surrounded by toast triangles spread with savoury butter. Serve with extra mushrooms and crisp bacon rolls.

# Vegetables

## Herb Pudding

*6 portions*

750g/$1\frac{1}{2}$lb mixed spring-green leaves (sorrel, cabbage, sprout tops, nettle, dandelion, beet tops, spinach)
2 medium-sized leeks, finely sliced
150g/5oz pearl barley
2 small eggs, beaten
$1\frac{1}{2}$ tablespoons each chopped parsley, thyme
salt, black pepper

Wash, trim and shred the green leaves and mix with the leeks. Put the vegetables with the pearl barley into a large muslin bag. Boil the bag in a large saucepan of boiling, salted water until the barley is tender. Empty the contents of the bag into a bowl. Stir in the eggs, herbs and seasoning and pile the mixture into a buttered ovenproof dish. Bake at 180°C/350°F/gas 4 for 30 minutes. Serve with roast meat and new potatoes.

# Boiled Spinach

*4 portions*

1kg/2lb spinach
salt, black pepper, grated nutmeg
15g/½oz butter

Pick over the spinach carefully and wash in several changes of water. Break off the stalks and remove the central ribs if coarse. Put the wet leaves into a large saucepan without any additional water and cook gently for 5 to 10 minutes until tender. Drain thoroughly in a colander and return to the pan. Add seasoning to taste and butter.

# Baked Stuffed Onions

*6 portions*

3 Spanish onions
40g/1½oz butter
50g/2oz chopped mushrooms
175g/6oz sausagemeat
4 tablespoons fresh breadcrumbs
1 teaspoon prepared mustard
salt, pepper
4 tablespoons stock

Peel the onions and boil them in water until just tender. Drain and cool. Scoop out the centres and chop for the stuffing. Heat 15g/½oz butter and fry the mushrooms. Mix the chopped onion centres, mushrooms, sausagemeat and breadcrumbs. Melt the remaining butter and add to the stuffing mixture with the mustard and seasoning. Pack into the onion shells using a teaspoon.

Place the stuffed onions in an ovenproof dish and pour the stock around them. Cover with a lid or foil. Bake at 180°C/350°F/gas 4 for 30 minutes, until the stuffing is cooked. Remove the lid or foil 10 minutes before the end of cooking time.

# Pease Pudding

*4 portions*

225g/8oz dried split yellow peas
50g/2oz butter
1 onion, chopped
salt, pepper
1 large egg, beaten
flour

Soak the dried peas in cold water overnight. Drain and rinse. Cover with cold water and bring slowly to the boil. Simmer gently for 2 to $2\frac{1}{2}$ hours until tender, then drain. Mash or sieve the peas.

Melt the butter, add the onion and fry until transparent. Add the pea purée, seasoning and egg. Sprinkle a pudding cloth with flour and place the pea mixture in it. Tie the cloth tightly, lower into a pan of boiling water and cook for 45 minutes. Turn out on to a hot dish and serve with bacon, pork, pork sausages or boiled beef.

Alternatively, bake the pease pudding in a buttered casserole, covered with a lid or foil, at 180°C/350°F/gas 4 for about 40 minutes.

# Mashed Swedes

*4 portions*

750g/1½lb swedes
750g/1½lb potatoes
1 litre/1¾ pints beef stock or water
salt, black pepper
¼ teaspoon ground allspice
15g/½oz butter

Peel the swedes and potatoes and cut into pieces. Bring the stock or water to the boil and add the swedes and seasonings. Cook until semi-tender. Add the potatoes and cook until the vegetables are tender. Drain off the liquid and mash the vegetables with the butter. Add a sprinkling of freshly milled pepper.

# Roast Parsnips

*4–6 portions*

750g/1½lb parsnips
50g/2oz butter or beef dripping
2 teaspoons lemon juice
salt, pepper
½ teaspoon dry mustard

Wash and scrub the parsnips. Trim off the tops. Scrape, if preferred. Cut into quarters. Parboil in boiling salted water for 10 minutes. Drain thoroughly. Set the oven at 180°C/350°F/gas 4 and heat the butter or dripping in an ovenproof dish. Add the parsnips and turn them in the fat. Sprinkle over the lemon juice and seasonings. Roast for 20 to 30 minutes until browned and tender.

Alternatively, roast the parboiled parsnips in the fatty meat juices of a roasting pan during the last 30 minutes of cooking a joint of beef or veal.

# Potato Chips

*4 portions*

750g/$1\frac{1}{2}$lb potatoes
oil for deep frying
salt

Select long, thin potatoes, if possible. Peel them and cut lengthways into uniform strips. Rinse in cold water, drain, dry on absorbent paper. Heat the oil to 177–182°C/350–360°F. Put the chips, a few at a time, into the frying basket and carefully lower them into the hot oil. Cook until the potatoes are softened but still pale in colour. Drain.

Reheat the oil to a hotter temperature, 188–199°C/370–390°F, and fry the chips a second time until they are golden brown and crisp. Drain on absorbent paper. Serve at once, sprinkled with salt.

# Baked Jacket Potatoes

*4 portions*

4–8 large floury potatoes
butter for serving

Select potatoes that are uniform in size. Scrub, rinse and dry the potatoes and make a small slit in one side of each potato. Place on a rack in the oven and bake at 200–220°C/400–425°F/gas 6–7 for about 1 hour. The potatoes should be soft when gently squeezed in a cloth. Slit the potatoes on top and insert a knob of butter. Serve at once.

# Fish

## Grilled Bloaters with Mustard Butter

*4 portions*

4 bloaters
1 teaspoon lemon juice
black pepper
mustard butter, $\frac{1}{2}$ quantity (see page 78)
1 lemon, cut into wedges

Clean the bloaters and remove the heads. Wash and pat dry with absorbent paper. Score 2 or 3 times on each side. Line the grill rack with foil and heat the grill. Add the lemon juice and pepper to the mustard butter and insert a spoonful into each scored slit in the fish.

Grill the fish for about 5 minutes on each side, turning them carefully. Arrange on a hot serving dish and spoon over the juices from the foil. Serve garnished with lemon wedges, with crusty bread and butter.

# Mackerel with Gooseberry Sauce

*4 portions*

Clean the mackerel and remove the heads. Wash and pat dry with absorbent paper. Sprinkle the gut cavities with seasoning. Line the grill rack with foil and heat the grill. Brush the surface of each fish with oil and grill for about 8 minutes on each side.

Meanwhile, rinse, top and tail the gooseberries and simmer them in the water until tender. Sieve the cooked berries, or purée them in an electric blender. Add the sugar and lemon rind and reheat the sauce.

Serve the fish with the sauce and with boiled potatoes.

4 mackerel
salt, pepper
oil for grilling

*Gooseberry Sauce*
225g/8oz green gooseberries
150ml/$\frac{1}{4}$ pint water
1 tablespoon sugar
grated rind $\frac{1}{2}$ lemon

# Fried Herrings in Oatmeal

*4 portions*

Scale and clean the herrings, and remove the heads and fins. Wash and pat dry with absorbent paper. Dip the fish into well-seasoned oatmeal. The roes may also be rinsed, dried, coated and fried. Fry in shallow fat on both sides until cooked and browned, 10 to 15 minutes in all. Garnish with lemon wedges and serve with boiled potatoes.

4 herrings
50g/2oz coarse or medium oatmeal
salt, pepper
butter or bacon fat for frying
1 lemon, cut into wedges

# Grilled Herrings with Mustard Sauce

*4 portions*

- 4 herrings
- 1 tablespoon lemon juice
- salt, black pepper
- melted butter or oil for grilling
- mustard sauce (see page 73)
- 2 tablespoons chopped parsley
- 1 lemon, cut into wedges

Clean the herrings and remove the heads and fins. Wash and pat dry with absorbent paper. Season inside with lemon juice, salt and pepper. Lightly score both sides of each fish with two oblique cuts. Line the grill rack with foil and heat the grill. Put the fish on the rack, brush them with melted butter or oil and grill until lightly browned. Turn the fish, brush them with more melted butter or oil and grill until cooked and browned.

Meanwhile prepare the mustard sauce. Arrange the grilled fish on a hot serving dish. Garnish with chopped parsley and lemon wedges. Serve with boiled potatoes and the mustard sauce.

# Baked Soused Herrings

*3 portions*

- 6 herrings
- 1–2 tablespoons prepared mustard
- salt, black pepper
- 6 pickled gherkins
- 1 blade mace
- 1 teaspoon pickling spice
- 3 or 4 cloves
- 2 bay leaves
- 1 or 2 small onions, thinly sliced
- 150ml/$\frac{1}{4}$ pint malt vinegar
- 150ml/$\frac{1}{4}$ pint water
- sprigs parsley (optional)

Scale and clean the herrings and remove the heads, tails and fins. Wash and pat dry with absorbent paper. Split and bone them. Season the flat fillets lightly on the fleshy side with mustard, salt and pepper. Roll up each fillet around a pickled gherkin, skin side out, starting at the tail end of the fillet.

Pack the herrings neatly together in an ovenproof dish and add the mace, pickling spice, cloves and bay leaves. Top with the onion slices and pour over the vinegar and water so that the fish is just covered with the liquid. Cover the dish and bake at 180°C/350°F/gas 4 for 45 minutes. Serve the herrings cooled in the cooking juices, garnished with parsley if you like, with salad and boiled potatoes.

# Grilled Kippers

*4 portions*

The kippers may be grilled whole or headless. Line the grill rack with foil and heat the grill. Lay the kippers skin side up on the rack and grill for about 3 minutes. Turn the kippers over, dot each one with a piece of butter and grill for a further 3 minutes, lowering the heat if necessary. Serve at once, garnished with lemon wedges, with brown bread and butter or toast.

4–8 kippers
butter for grilling
1 lemon, cut into wedges

# Stewed Eels

*6 portions*

Wash and skin the eels. Cut them into pieces 10cm/4 inches long. Put them in a shallow, heavy pan. Add the stock, spices, parsley, lemon and onion, and salt if required. Cover and simmer very gently until the eels are tender, about 30 to 40 minutes. Lift out the eels with a fish slice and transfer them to a hot dish. Strain the stock.

Melt the butter in a saucepan and add the flour. Cook gently for 2 to 3 minutes, stirring. Gradually add the stock and bring to the boil, stirring constantly. Simmer for 5 minutes. Add the port or sherry and the mustard. Pour the sauce over the eels and serve hot with creamed potatoes or crusty bread.

1kg/2lb eels
400ml/¾ pint beef stock
5 grains allspice
6 peppercorns
2 cloves
1 blade mace
4 sprigs parsley
¼ lemon
1 onion, quartered
salt (optional)
25g/1oz butter
1½ tablespoons flour
5 tablespoons port or sherry
2 teaspoons prepared mustard

# Fried Whitebait

*4 portions*

450g/1lb whitebait
flour for coating
salt, pepper
oil for deep frying
sprigs parsley
1 lemon, cut into quarters

Rinse the whitebait carefully. Drain well and dry the fish on absorbent paper. Toss gently in lightly seasoned flour, place the fish in a sieve and shake off surplus flour.

Heat the oil to 190°C/375°F. Fry the whitebait in small batches in a finely meshed frying basket for 2 to 3 minutes until crisply cooked. Shake the basket periodically if the whitebait tend to cling together during frying. Drain the basket thoroughly when each batch is fried. Turn the whitebait on to absorbent paper and keep them hot in a serving dish until all are fried.

Carefully fry a few well dried sprigs of parsley for a few seconds and drain on absorbent paper. Put the fish on heated plates, and sprinkle with salt and pepper. Garnish with fried parsley sprigs and lemon quarters, and serve with thinly sliced brown bread and butter.

# Lakeland Fish Pie

*6 portions*

750g/1½lb smoked haddock fillet
50g/2oz butter
100g/4oz finely chopped onion
50g/2oz flour
2 teaspoons dry mustard
400ml/¾ pint milk
2–3 teaspoons lemon juice
3 hard-boiled eggs, chopped
salt, pepper

Poach the fish gently in water for about 12 minutes. Drain, remove any scum, bones and skin, and flake the fish. Melt the butter in a heavy pan and gently fry the onions. Stir in the flour and mustard and cook for 2 to 3 minutes. Remove from the heat and slowly stir in the milk. Return to the heat and stir constantly until the sauce comes to the boil. Simmer for 3 minutes. Stir in the lemon juice, the chopped hard-boiled eggs and the fish. Season to taste and pile the mixture into a large shallow baking dish.

To make the topping, put the flour into a bowl. Add seasoning and rub in the butter. Mix in the cheese. Sprinkle the mixture over the contents of the baking dish. Bake at 180°C/350°F/gas 4 for 30 to 40 minutes, until the topping is crisp and brown. Serve hot with a cooked green vegetable such as broccoli.

*Topping*
100g/4oz flour
salt, pepper
50g/2oz butter
75g/3oz finely grated Cheddar cheese

# Kedgeree

*4 portions*

Cook the rice in boiling salted water for 15 to 20 minutes until tender. Poach the fish gently in the milk and water for about 12 minutes. Drain, remove any scum, bones and skin, and flake the fish. When the rice is cooked, rinse it under cold running water and drain.

Melt the butter. Add the fish and rice. Add the chopped hard-boiled eggs and seasoning. Heat the mixture carefully, turning with a fork. Stir in half the parsley. Turn the kedgeree on to a heated serving dish and sprinkle with the rest of the parsley. Serve hot as a breakfast or supper dish.

175g/6oz long-grain rice
450g/1lb smoked haddock fillet
150ml/¼ pint milk
150ml/¼ pint water
50g/2oz butter
2 hard-boiled eggs, chopped
salt, pepper
4 tablespoons chopped parsley

# Fish Cakes

*4 portions*

350g/12oz cooked fish fillet (cod, coley or haddock)
450g/1lb freshly boiled, mashed potatoes
3 tablespoons milk
25g/1oz butter
2 eggs, beaten
salt, white pepper
1 teaspoon prepared mustard
flour for coating
golden breadcrumbs
oil for frying
sprigs parsley
1 lemon, cut into wedges

Flake the cooked fish finely. Mix the mashed potatoes with the milk, butter, 1 beaten egg, salt, pepper and mustard. Stir in the flaked fish. Shape the mixture into a roll on a floured board. Cut into 8 slices. Season the remaining beaten egg. Dip each slice into flour, then into egg and finally into breadcrumbs. Heat the oil in a heavy frying pan. Fry the cakes on both sides until golden brown. Drain on absorbent paper. Serve garnished with parsley sprigs and lemon wedges.

# Dressed Crab

*4 portions*

Twist off the claws of each crab, keeping the small leg claws for decoration. Cut the tendons at the base of the large pincer claws. Crack the shell part of the claws using a heavy knife blade, remove the meat and shred it into a bowl.

Turn each crab on to its shell, lift up the apron and remove it. Pick out the white meat and add it to the claw meat. Discard the sac in the shell near the head, also the gills and any green matter. Put the brown meat into a second bowl and any remaining white meat into the first bowl. Gently tap the inside edge of the shell to break it along the line which is naturally demarcated. Wash and dry the shell thoroughly and rub lightly with a little oil.

Make the dressing by mixing the oil and seasoning and adding the vinegar gradually, stirring constantly. Divide between the white and brown meats. Add the breadcrumbs to the brown meat. Arrange the white meat on either side of each shell, with a strip of brown meat in the centre. Sieve the egg yolk and use to decorate, with parsley and paprika.

2 crabs
25g/1oz fresh breadcrumbs
1 hard-boiled egg yolk
2 tablespoons chopped parsley
paprika pepper

*Dressing*
3 tablespoons oil
salt, pepper, dry mustard
1 tablespoon vinegar

# Devilled Crab

*4 portions*

50g/2oz fresh breadcrumbs
100ml/4fl oz milk
150g/5oz flaked crab meat (freshly boiled or canned)
2 egg yolks
75g/3oz butter, melted
1 tablespoon prepared mustard
large pinch ground mace
salt, pepper
2 tablespoons chopped parsley
lemon slices
watercress sprigs

*Topping*
15–20g/½–¾oz fresh breadcrumbs
1 tablespoon chopped parsley
15g/½oz butter

Soak the breadcrumbs in the milk before mixing with the crab meat. Stir in the egg yolks, melted butter, seasonings and parsley. Pile the mixture into cleaned, oiled scallop or crab shells. Sprinkle breadcrumbs and parsley on top and dot with butter.

Bake at 230°C/450°F/gas 8 for 10 to 15 minutes until well browned. Garnish with lemon slices and watercress sprigs. Serve hot as a starter or as a light luncheon or supper dish accompanied by a green salad.

# Potted Shrimps

*4 portions*

175g/6oz butter
1 litre/1¾ pints cooked shrimps, peeled
½ teaspoon black pepper
¼ teaspoon salt
¼ teaspoon ground mace
½ teaspoon dry mustard

Melt 100g/4oz butter in a heavy saucepan and when foaming (but not browned) add the shrimps. Add the seasonings and toss the shrimps lightly in the butter until thoroughly heated but not fried. Put the mixture into small pots. Melt the rest of the butter and pour into the pots to seal. Allow to cool and set. Cover the pots with cling-film. Store in a cool place or in the refrigerator for up to 6 days. Serve with hot toast.

*Opposite: Devilled crab (recipe above).*
*Overleaf: Baked soused herrings (recipe page 28).*

Colman's
DIJON
MUSTARD

# Meat, Poultry & Game

## Roast Beef

*6 portions*

Wipe the meat with a damp cloth. Rub with salt and pepper, then dredge lightly with flour. Heat dripping in a roasting tin and place meat in tin, fatty side uppermost. Roast at 200°C/400°F/gas 6 for 8 to 10 minutes, then reduce the heat to 170°C/325°F/gas 3 until cooked. For medium-rare meat, allow 1 hour 10 minutes for the rolled rib or fillet and 1 hour 45 minutes for the sirloin. Remove the meat to a warm serving dish and keep hot while making the gravy.

Drain off fat from the tin and sprinkle enough flour into the tin to absorb the remaining meat juices. Brown this mixture, then stir in the vegetable stock or water, bring to the boil and season to taste.

Serve the beef with the gravy, roast potatoes, a green vegetable, Yorkshire pudding (see overleaf), horseradish sauce (see page 74) and mustard.

1kg/2lb rolled boned rib of beef or 1 whole fillet of beef or 1.5kg/3lb sirloin of beef
2 teaspoons salt
pepper
flour
50g/2oz dripping
300ml/½ pint vegetable water or stock

# Yorkshire Pudding

*6 portions*

100g/4oz flour
pinch salt
1 egg, lightly beaten
300ml/$\frac{1}{2}$ pint milk
25g/1oz dripping

Sift the flour and salt into a bowl. Make a well in the centre and add the egg, then half the milk. Stir, drawing in the flour from the sides. Beat well until smooth. Beat in the rest of the milk.

Put the dripping in a Yorkshire pudding tin 23 × 15cm/9 × 6 inches and heat in the oven at 220°C/425°F/gas 7 until the dripping is just beginning to smoke. Stir the batter and pour it into the tin. Bake for 35 to 40 minutes until well risen and golden.

# Boiled Beef and Dumplings

*6–8 portions*

1–1.5 kg/2–3lb salt silverside of beef
1 bouquet garni
6 black peppercorns
750g/1$\frac{1}{2}$lb onions
750g/1$\frac{1}{2}$lb carrots, halved lengthwise

*Dumplings*
100g/4oz self-raising flour
40g/1$\frac{1}{2}$oz shredded suet
1 tablespoon chopped parsley
1 tablespoon finely chopped onion
4–5 tablespoons cold water

Soak the meat for 1 hour in cold water. Put it into a large saucepan, cover with fresh cold water, bring to boiling point and skim. Add the bouquet garni and peppercorns, cover and simmer for 1$\frac{1}{4}$ hours. Add the onions and carrots and simmer for a further 45 minutes until the vegetables are tender.

Meanwhile mix together the flour, suet, parsley and onion. Mix to a firm dough with water. Divide into 8 to 12 balls. Simmer with the meat for 15 to 20 minutes. Serve the meat on a hot dish and arrange the vegetables, dumplings and a little of the cooking liquid around. Accompany with boiled potatoes, mustard and horseradish sauce (see page 74).

# Beef Olives

*4 portions*

750g/$1\frac{1}{2}$lb topside of beef
2 teaspoons prepared mustard
flour for coating
salt, pepper
1 onion, sliced
1 carrot, sliced
50g/2oz dripping
300ml/$\frac{1}{2}$ pint water

*Forcemeat*
15g/$\frac{1}{2}$oz fresh breadcrumbs
25g/1oz shredded suet
1 teaspoon dried mixed herbs
1 tablespoon chopped parsley
grated rind 1 lemon
1 egg, beaten
salt, pepper

Remove fat from the beef and cut the meat into very thin slices about 7.5 × 10cm/3 × 4 inches. Flatten the slices by beating with a rolling pin. Spread each slice with mustard.

Mix together all the ingredients for the forcemeat, put a little on each slice of meat and roll it up. Tie each 'olive' with white thread or fine kitchen string. Coat the olives with seasoned flour. Toss the vegetables in the flour.

Heat the dripping in a heavy pan. Fry the olives in the fat until nicely browned all over, then remove to an ovenproof casserole. Brown the vegetables in the same fat and add them to the casserole. Add the water to the pan and scrape up the pan juices to make a gravy. Season to taste and pour into the casserole.

Cover and cook in the oven at 190°C/375°F/gas 5 for $1\frac{1}{2}$ to 2 hours. Alternatively, simmer in a heavy saucepan over a low top heat for 2 to $2\frac{1}{2}$ hours. Serve with creamed potatoes.

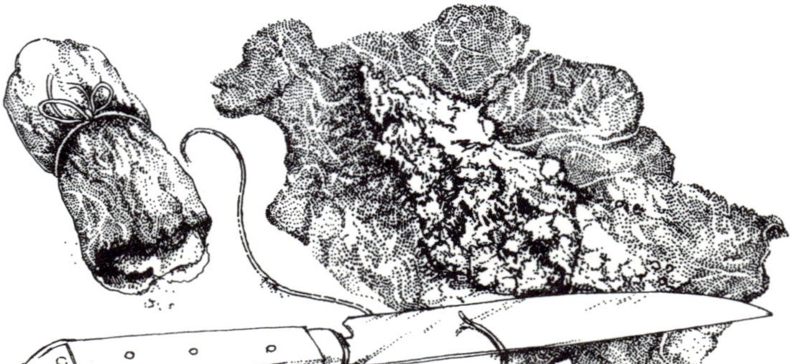

# Norfolk Stew

*3–4 portions*

450g/1lb braising steak
25g/1oz flour
2 teaspoons dry mustard
salt, pepper
40g/1½oz dripping
2 onions, sliced
225g/8oz carrots, sliced
2 or 3 sticks celery, sliced
400ml/¾ pint beef stock
1 bay leaf

Remove excess fat from the steak and cut the meat into cubes. Season the flour with the mustard and a little salt and pepper. Roll the meat in the flour.

Melt the dripping in a large saucepan over a low heat, lightly brown the meat, add the vegetables and fry for a few more minutes. Add any remaining flour. Pour in the stock and add the bay leaf. Cover and simmer for 2½ hours or cook in a casserole in the oven at 180°C/350°F/gas 4 for the same length of time. Remove the bay leaf before serving.

# English Club Steak and Kidney Pie

*4 portions*

350g/12oz chuck steak
1 lamb's kidney
1 tablespoon flour
salt, pepper
50g/2oz sliced mushrooms
pinch dried mixed herbs
2 teaspoons prepared mustard
80ml/3fl oz water
200g/7oz packet frozen puff pastry, thawed
milk for glazing

Trim the steak and cut into cubes. Cut the kidney into small pieces, removing the core. Season the flour and roll the steak and kidney in it, then place in a casserole dish. Add the mushrooms, herbs, mustard and water. Cover and cook for 2½ hours at 180°C/350°F/gas 4 or simmer in a saucepan with a tight-fitting lid for the same length of time. Allow to cool, then transfer to a deep pie plate.

Roll out the pastry a little larger all round than the pie plate. Moisten the rim of the plate. Cut off a strip of pastry and place around rim of plate. Moisten the strip. Cover with the remaining pastry. Trim and knock up the edges. Make a hole in the centre of the pastry to allow steam to escape. Decorate with leaves made from pastry scraps. Brush with milk.

Set the pie plate on a baking sheet and bake at 220°C/425°F/gas 7 for about 20 minutes.

# Cornish Pasties

*6 pasties*

Trim and finely chop the beef, and mix with the potatoes, onion, water and seasoning. Roll out the pastry on a floured board and cut it into 6 rounds about 15cm/6 inches in diameter. Divide the filling evenly between the pastry rounds, dampen the edges and press together at the top, making large flutes. Brush with milk. Bake at 200°C/400°F/gas 6 for 30 minutes, then reduce the heat to 190°C/375°F/gas 5 and cook for a further 15 minutes or until the meat is cooked.

350g/12oz stewing beef
350g/12oz potatoes, finely diced
1 medium-sized onion, finely chopped
1 tablespoon water
salt, pepper
shortcrust pastry, using 225g/8oz flour etc (see page 15)
milk for glazing

# Steak and Kidney Pudding

*4 portions*

Grease a 900ml/1½ pint pudding basin. Roll out the pastry into a circle large enough to fill the basin, then cut out a quarter. Place the remaining three quarters of the circle in the basin, joining the cut edges securely.

Trim and cube the meat. Cut the kidneys into small pieces, removing the cores. Roll the steak and kidney in flour seasoned with salt, pepper and mustard and add with the onion and mushrooms to the lined basin. Pour the water over, moisten the edge of the pastry and cover with the remaining pastry rolled out to make a lid. Seal the edges and cover with greased greaseproof paper and foil. Steam for 3 hours. Remove foil and paper. Turn the pudding out on to a hot dish. Garnish with parsley or watercress.

suet crust pastry (see overleaf)
350g/12oz chuck steak
4 lambs' kidneys
flour for coating
salt, pepper
½ teaspoon dry mustard
1 onion, chopped
50g/2oz sliced mushrooms
150ml/¼ pint water
sprigs parsley or watercress

# Suet Crust Pastry

225g/8oz self-raising flour
$\frac{1}{2}$ teaspoon salt
100g/4oz shredded suet
about 150ml/$\frac{1}{4}$ pint cold water

Sift together the flour and the salt. Stir in the suet. Mix to a firm dough with water, and use as required.

# Savoury Beef Roll

*4 portions*

suet crust pastry (see above)
350g/12oz minced beef
1 onion, chopped
25–50g/1–2oz chopped mushrooms
$\frac{1}{4}$ teaspoon dried mixed herbs
2 teaspoons prepared mustard
1 tablespoon water
salt, pepper

Roll out the pastry on a lightly floured surface to form a rectangle 22 × 25cm/8$\frac{1}{2}$ × 10 inches. Mix the minced beef with the onion, mushrooms, herbs, mustard, water and a little salt and pepper. Spread the filling over the pastry, leaving 1cm/$\frac{1}{2}$ inch clear round the edge as the filling will spread out when rolled up. Roll one long edge towards the other long edge. Place in a greased piece of foil, fold the ends to secure. Steam for 2$\frac{3}{4}$ hours. Serve with gravy or a tomato sauce.

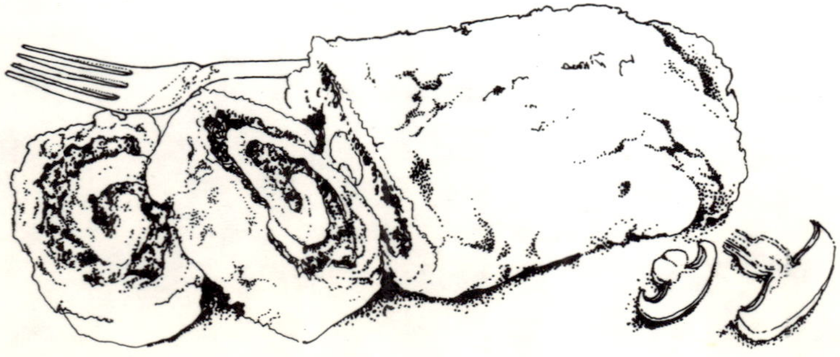

# Raised Veal and Ham Pie

*6 portions*

Cut off one third of the pastry for the lid. Mould the rest over a large oiled jam jar. Leave to cool, then remove the jam jar. Keep the pastry for the lid warm while preparing the filling.

Cut the veal into 2.5cm/1 inch cubes. Mix together the seasonings, lemon rind and parsley. Dip the veal and ham in this mixture, then arrange the meat in the pastry crust with the eggs. Add 4 tablespoons stock. Roll out the pastry for the lid a little larger than the top of the pie case. Moisten the top edges of the pie case. Cover with the pastry lid and seal the edges. Make a hole in the top of the lid and brush with beaten egg.

Bake at 230°C/450°F/gas 8 for about 20 minutes, until beginning to brown. Reduce the heat to 180°C/350°F/gas 4, cover with greaseproof paper and cook for about 2½ hours. Allow to cool.

Mix the gelatine with 3 tablespoons stock in a small jug. Bring the remaining stock to the boil and pour it into the jug. Stir and allow to cool. When it is just on the point of setting, pour into the pie through the hole in the top.

hot water crust pastry (see below)
750g/1½lb lean pie veal
1 teaspoon salt
½ teaspoon pepper
1 teaspoon dry mustard
1 teaspoon grated lemon rind
1 teaspoon chopped parsley
225g/8oz diced ham
2 hard-boiled eggs, quartered
200ml/7fl oz stock
beaten egg for glazing
1½ teaspoons gelatine

# Hot Water Crust Pastry

Sift the flour and salt into a warm bowl. Melt the lard in the water and bring to the boil. Pour into the flour and mix thoroughly. Turn the dough on to a lightly floured surface and knead until smooth. Return it to the bowl, cover and leave to stand in a warm place for 30 minutes. Use while still warm.

350g/12oz flour
1 teaspoon salt
100g/4oz lard
150ml/¼ pint water

# Shepherd's Pie

*4 portions*

450g/1lb cold cooked lamb or beef
25g/1oz dripping or butter
1 onion, chopped
25g/1oz flour
300ml/$\frac{1}{2}$ pint stock or water
1 tablespoon tomato purée
1 teaspoon prepared mustard
salt, pepper
850g/1$\frac{3}{4}$lb potatoes, peeled
40g/1$\frac{1}{2}$oz butter
hot milk
sprigs parsley

Mince the meat very finely. Heat the fat in a heavy saucepan and fry the onion until transparent. Sprinkle the flour over the onion and cook for 2 minutes. Remove from the heat and slowly stir in the stock or water, tomato purée and mustard. Season to taste with salt and pepper. Bring to the boil, stirring constantly, and simmer for 3 minutes. Remove from the heat and allow to cool.

Meanwhile boil the potatoes in lightly salted water until tender. Drain and mash them, beating in half the butter and a little hot milk, until light and fluffy. Season to taste.

Put the meat into a shallow, well-buttered ovenproof dish and pour over the sauce. Spread the potato mixture on top and decorate using the prongs of a fork. Dot with the rest of the butter. Bake at 220°C/425°F/gas 7 for 20 minutes, or until heated through and nicely browned on top. Serve garnished with sprigs of parsley.

*Note:* This dish may also be prepared using uncooked meat. You will need 750g/1$\frac{1}{2}$lb finely minced lamb or beef. When the onion is almost transparent, add the meat to the pan and fry lightly until the meat changes colour. Transfer the meat and onions to the ovenproof dish and add another 25g/1oz dripping or butter to the pan before sprinkling in flour and making sauce as directed.

*Opposite: Kedgeree (recipe page 31).*
*Overleaf: Chicken pie (recipe page 60).*

THE
MUSTARD

ALE'S
HONEY

# Cumbrian Tatie Pot

*4 portions*

Trim the meat, cut it into pieces and put it in a baking dish. Add the black pudding, onion and carrot. Top with the potato slices arranged in an overlapping fashion. Mix the stock with the mustard and pour over the dish. Sprinkle with seasoning. Cover and bake at 180°C/350°F/gas 4 for about 2 hours. Remove the lid. Dust the potatoes with a little seasoned flour and cook for a further 30 minutes to brown the top.

750g/$1\frac{1}{2}$lb boned middle neck of mutton or shin of beef
1 coil black pudding, sliced
1 onion, chopped
1 carrot, chopped
1kg/2lb potatoes, sliced
600ml/1 pint stock
2 teaspoons prepared mustard
salt, pepper
flour

# Honey Glazed Pork

*6–8 portions*

Ask the butcher to score the pork rind. Place the joint on a trivet in a roasting tin, rub seasoning and honey over the whole surface and brush with oil. Stick cloves into the rind. Roast at 220°C/425°F/gas 7 for 40 minutes. Reduce the oven temperature to 180°C/350°F/gas 4 and cook for a further 2 hours. Baste the joint 3 or 4 times during cooking.

Heat the apricots in their syrup, and drain just before serving. Transfer the joint to a hot dish and serve with the apricot halves. Garnish with sage leaves.

2kg/4lb leg of pork
salt, pepper
2 teaspoons dry mustard
4 tablespoons honey
about 2 tablespoons oil
12–24 cloves
1kg/2lb canned apricot halves
sage leaves

*Previous page: Oxford kidneys (recipe page 54).*
*Opposite: Honey glazed pork (recipe above).*

# Pork and Apple Casserole

*4–6 portions*

25g/1oz flour
2 tablespoons dry mustard
salt, pepper
1kg/2lb boned blade or shoulder of pork
50g/2oz butter
2 tablespoons oil
2 onions, thinly sliced
300ml/½ pint light stock
300ml/½ pint cider
1 teaspoon dried sage
1 teaspoon dried thyme
3 cloves
450g/1lb apples

Put the flour and mustard in a bowl and season with salt and pepper. Cut the pork into cubes and toss them in the seasoned flour. Heat the butter and oil in a heavy pan and fry the onions until soft. Add the pork and fry until golden brown. Stir in any excess flour. Add the stock, cider, herbs and cloves. Bring to the boil, reduce the heat, cover the pan and simmer gently for 1½ hours.

Core and thickly slice the apples and add these to the pan. Cook for a further 30 minutes. (The casserole can, alternatively, be cooked in the oven at 180°C/350°F/gas 4.) Serve with plain boiled potatoes and carrots or a green vegetable.

# Steamed Bacon Pudding

*4 portions*

- suet crust pastry (see page 42)
- 450g/1lb gammon, cubed
- 1 large onion, sliced
- 3 teaspoons prepared mustard
- ½ teaspoon dried mixed herbs
- salt, pepper
- 1 tablespoon water

Grease a 900ml/1½ pint pudding basin. Roll out the pastry into a circle large enough to fill the basin, then cut out a quarter. Place the remaining three quarters of the circle in the basin, joining the cut edges securely.

In a separate basin mix together the gammon, onion, mustard, herbs and seasoning. Place in the lined pudding basin. Add the water. Moisten the edge of the pastry and cover with the remaining pastry rolled out to make a lid. Seal the edges and cover with greased greaseproof paper and foil. Steam for 3 hours. Remove foil and paper. Turn out on to a hot dish and serve with a green vegetable.

# Toad-in-the-hole

*4–6 portions*

- 200g/7oz flour
- large pinch salt
- 2 eggs, lightly beaten
- 600ml/1 pint milk
- 450–750g/1–1½lb pork sausages

Sift the flour and salt into a bowl. Make a well in the centre and add the eggs, then half the milk. Stir, drawing in the flour from the sides. Beat well until smooth. Beat in the rest of the milk.

Grease a Yorkshire pudding tin and arrange the sausages in it. Cook them in the oven at 220°C/425°F/gas 7 for 15 minutes. Pour the batter over the sausages and bake for 35 to 40 minutes until crisp and golden.

# Sausage Rolls

*14–16 rolls*

750g/1½lb sausagemeat
rough puff pastry, using 225g/8oz flour etc (see below)
prepared mustard
milk or beaten egg for glazing

Divide the sausagemeat into 2 portions. Roll each into a 36cm/14 inch long roll. Roll out pastry thinly to an oblong 36 × 25cm/14 × 10 inches, then cut in half making 2 long strips 36 × 12.5cm/14 × 5 inches. Brush the long edges with water. Smear each strip with mustard and put a sausage 'roll' on to each strip. Wrap the pastry over and join the edges, leaving the ends open. Cut each roll into 7 or 8 and make 2 diagonal cuts across the top of each.

Place on baking sheets and brush with milk or beaten egg. Bake at 230°C/450°F/gas 8 for 20 to 25 minutes. Cool on a wire rack. Sausage rolls are best eaten while fresh and warm, with a salad.

# Rough Puff Pastry

100g/4oz flour
pinch salt
75g/3oz butter
1½ teaspoons lemon juice
about 5 tablespoons cold water

Sift together the flour and salt. Add the butter cut up roughly into 1cm/½ inch cubes and mix lightly. Add the lemon juice and enough water to form a soft dough. Cover with a polythene bag and put in a cool place for 15 to 30 minutes.

Roll out to an oblong strip 10–13cm/4–5 inches wide and about 5mm/¼ inch thick. Mark very lightly into three. Fold each outer third over the middle, press the edges lightly and then turn the pastry through a right angle. Roll out into a strip as before and fold again. Wrap in a polythene bag and set aside in a cool place for 15 to 20 minutes. Roll out and fold twice more, then use as required.

# Ox Tongue

*8–10 portions*

1.5–1.75kg/3–3½lb pickled ox tongue
2 onions
2 carrots
3 sticks celery (including leaves)
1 bay leaf
3 sprigs parsley
1 sprig thyme
3–4 cloves
10 peppercorns
mustard sauce (see page 73) or Cumberland sauce (see page 74) (optional)

Wash the tongue thoroughly and soak in cold water for 3 to 4 hours. Rinse and place in a large saucepan. Cover with water and add the vegetables, herbs and spices. Bring slowly to the boil, removing scum as it forms. Cover and simmer gently for about 3 hours until tender. Add extra water if necessary to keep the tongue covered. Allow the tongue to cool in the cooking liquid just sufficiently to handle. Discard all the small bones, excess fat and gristle from the root end of the tongue and peel off the skin.

The tongue may be served hot, sliced from the root end to the tip, with mustard sauce or Cumberland sauce and vegetables, or it may be pressed for serving cold.

To press the tongue, curl it round to fit into a large round cake tin or deep dish. Pour in sufficient strained cooking liquid to cover the tongue. Place a layer of foil or a large plate over the tin or dish and weight it down. Leave in a cold place overnight so that the gelatinous stock sets firmly. Turn out the tongue and serve sliced, with mustard, redcurrant jelly, jacket potatoes and a green salad.

# Creamed Sweetbreads

*4 portions*

450g/1lb calf's or lamb's sweetbreads
2 teaspoons vinegar
1 teaspoon salt
50g/2oz butter
50g/2oz flour
pepper
300ml/$\frac{1}{2}$ pint veal or chicken stock
300ml/$\frac{1}{2}$ pint milk
2 teaspoons lemon juice
2 teaspoons prepared mustard
2 tablespoons chopped parsley
2 tablespoons Marsala or sherry

*Garnish*
4 large slices bread
75g/3oz butter
1 tablespoon chopped parsley

Soak the sweetbreads in water for 1 hour. Rinse, place them in a saucepan. Cover with cold water, add the vinegar and the salt and bring slowly to the boil. Simmer for 15 to 20 minutes. Drain and rinse under cold running water. Remove membranes and fat.

Melt the butter for the sauce. Stir in the flour and cook for 2 to 3 minutes without colouring. Add salt and pepper. Remove from the heat and gradually add the stock and milk, stirring constantly. Return to the heat and bring to the boil, still stirring. Add the lemon juice, mustard and parsley and simmer for about 5 minutes. Add the Marsala or sherry and the sweetbreads and reheat the sauce but do not boil. Taste for seasoning and adjust if necessary.

Prepare the garnish by cutting a round or crescent out of each slice of bread. Heat the butter in a frying pan and fry the bread shapes until golden. Transfer the creamed sweetbreads to a hot serving dish and garnish with the fried bread and chopped parsley.

# Oxford Kidneys

*4 portions*

12 lambs' kidneys
75g/3oz butter
1 tablespoon finely chopped onion
150ml/$\frac{1}{4}$ pint dry white wine
1 tablespoon lemon juice
1$\frac{1}{2}$ tablespoons prepared mustard

Slice the kidneys in half lengthways and remove the core. Heat 50g/2oz butter in a frying pan. Sauté the kidneys in the hot butter for 5 minutes, turning them frequently. Do not overcook. The kidneys should stiffen and brown slightly without becoming hard and dry. Remove to a hot plate.

Add the onion to the frying pan and sauté until soft and transparent. Add the wine and the lemon juice, turn up the heat, and boil until the liquid has reduced to about two thirds. Mash the mustard and the remaining butter. Remove the sauce from the heat and stir in the mustard butter in spoonfuls. Return the kidneys to the sauce together with any juices which may have drained from them. Reheat without boiling.

Serve the kidneys on boiled rice with the sauce poured over them, accompanied by a green salad.

# Liver and Onion Casserole

*4 portions*

- 450g/1lb lamb's liver, sliced
- flour for coating
- salt, pepper
- 25g/1oz butter
- 2 teaspoons dry mustard
- 100g/4oz fresh breadcrumbs
- 3 onions, thinly sliced
- 300ml/$\frac{1}{2}$ pint stock
- 2 tablespoons chopped parsley

Toss the sliced liver in seasoned flour. Melt the butter in a pan and quickly brown the liver; do not overcook. Mix the mustard with the breadcrumbs. Place a layer of liver at the bottom of a casserole, cover with a layer of breadcrumbs and then a layer of onion. Repeat, seasoning with salt and pepper between the layers, and finish with a layer of breadcrumbs.

Pour over the stock, cover and cook for $1\frac{1}{4}$ to $1\frac{1}{2}$ hours at 170°C/325°F/gas 3, until the liver is tender. Sprinkle with chopped parsley and serve with green vegetables.

# Stuffed Hearts

*4–6 portions*

8 lambs' hearts
100g/4oz fresh breadcrumbs
3–4 teaspoons dry mustard
2 teaspoons dried sage
salt, pepper
75g/3oz butter
3 medium-sized onions, chopped
300ml/½ pint stock
1 tablespoon cornflour
2 tablespoons cold water

Soak the hearts in cold water for 30 minutes. Put the breadcrumbs into a large basin. Sift the mustard over the crumbs. Add the sage and seasoning. Melt 50g/2oz butter and lightly fry a third of the onions in it. Add the onion and butter to the breadcrumbs. Fill the hearts with the stuffing. Sew up the top of each heart with white thread, using a large needle.

Melt the remaining butter in a large frying pan. Lightly brown the hearts on all sides, then transfer them to a deep ovenproof casserole. Fry the remaining onions until transparent. Add to the hearts. Pour the stock into the casserole, cover and cook gently at 170°C/325°F/gas 3 for 1½ to 2 hours until tender.

Remove the cotton thread and place the hearts and onions on a warmed serving dish. Pour the stock into a saucepan. Blend the cornflour to a paste with the cold water. Add a little stock to the paste and return to the pan. Bring to the boil, stirring constantly. Cook for 2 to 3 minutes. Pour over the hearts.

# Tripe and Onions

*4–6 portions*

1kg/2lb dressed tripe
450g/1lb onions, quartered
600ml/1 pint milk
salt, pepper
25g/1oz flour
2–3 tablespoons milk or water
3 tablespoons chopped parsley

Put the tripe into cold water and bring to the boil Drain and cut into 5cm/2 inch squares. Put the onions into cold water and bring to the boil. Drain and chop finely. Put the tripe, onions, milk and seasoning in a heavy saucepan, cover and simmer for 2 to 3 hours until the tripe is tender.

Mix the flour with the milk or water, add some of the hot milk from the saucepan, then stir the flour thickening into the pan. Simmer for 3 to 5 minutes, stirring. Adjust seasoning and add parsley.

Colman's
Mustard

# Roast Chicken

*4–6 portions*

2kg/4lb chicken
750ml/1¼ pints water
1 small onion, quartered
sprigs parsley
salt, pepper

*Stuffing*
100g/4oz fresh breadcrumbs
4 large spring onions, chopped
4 tablespoons chopped parsley
salt, pepper
grated rind and juice 1 lemon
100g/4oz butter, melted

*Sauce*
25g/1oz butter
1 tablespoon flour
¼ teaspoon lemon rind
1 teaspoon lemon juice
1 egg yolk, beaten

Simmer the chicken giblets in 600ml/1 pint water with the onion and parsley sprigs for about 1 hour. Strain and reserve the stock.

Mix together all the ingredients for the stuffing. Stuff the neck cavity of the chicken with the mixture. Place the chicken in a roasting tin. Pour over the remaining water and season the bird. Roast at 200°C/400°F/gas 6 for 1¼ hours, basting occasionally. Moisten further if necessary. Remove the chicken from the roasting tin and keep it warm. Strain the juices from the tin.

Prepare the sauce by melting the butter in the roasting tin and stirring in the flour. Add the stock from the giblets and the juices from the tin, the lemon rind and juice. Bring to the boil, stirring all the time, and cook for 1 to 2 minutes. Remove from the heat to cool slightly. Whisk in the beaten egg yolk. Reheat carefully, but do not allow the sauce to boil. Serve the carved chicken with the stuffing and sauce, and a selection of vegetables.

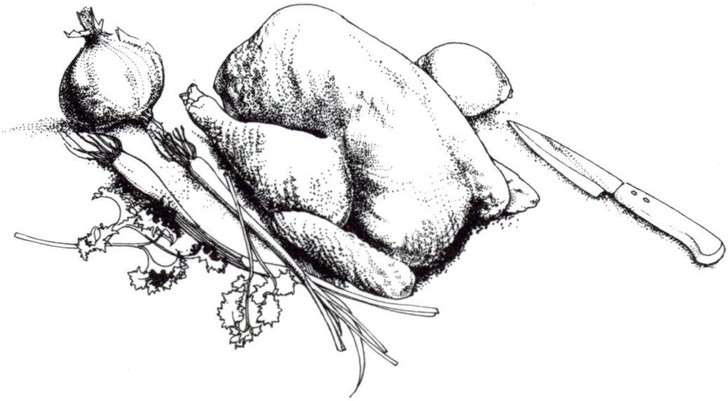

*Previous page: Sausage rolls (recipe page 52).*
*Opposite: Potted cheese (recipe page 68).*

# Chicken Pie

*6 portions*

1.5kg/3lb chicken, jointed
2 tablespoons flour
salt, pepper
50g/2oz butter
100g/4oz bacon, diced
1 medium-sized onion, sliced
100g/4oz mushrooms, sliced
1 tablespoon chopped parsley
½ teaspoon dried thyme
400ml/¾ pint stock or water
1 teaspoon prepared mustard
1 bay leaf
400g/14oz packet frozen puff pastry, thawed
milk for glazing

Wipe and dry the chicken, using absorbent paper. Toss in seasoned flour. Reserve the surplus flour for the sauce. Heat the butter in a large frying pan. Fry the bacon gently with the onion and mushrooms. Drain and set aside. Add the chicken joints to the pan and fry until browned on both sides. Put the chicken into a heavy casserole. Sprinkle over the fried onion, mushrooms and bacon, the parsley and thyme.

Add the rest of the coating flour to the fat in the frying pan. Stir over a low heat until browned. Remove from the heat and stir in the stock or water and the mustard. Return to the heat and cook slowly for 3 to 5 minutes, stirring constantly. Pour over the chicken and add the bay leaf.

Cover the casserole and cook at 180°C/350°F/gas 4 for 1¼ hours until tender. Allow the contents of the casserole to cool. Remove and discard the bay leaf. Remove skin and bones from the chicken joints. Cut the meat into 4cm/1½ inch pieces. Put the meat and sauce into a pie dish.

Roll out the pastry a little larger all round than the pie dish. Moisten the edge of the dish. Cut off a strip of pastry and place around edge of dish. Moisten the strip. Cover with the remaining pastry. Trim, knock up and flute the edges. Make a hole in the centre of the pastry to allow steam to escape. Decorate with leaves made from pastry scraps. Brush with milk.

Set the pie dish on a baking sheet and bake at 220°C/425°F/gas 7 for 35 to 40 minutes until the pastry is crisp and golden brown. Serve with vegetables.

# Roast Turkey

*6–8 portions hot, plus 6–8 portions cold*

- 4.5–5.5kg/10–12lb turkey
- 1 teaspoon salt
- 1 bay leaf
- sprigs parsley
- 6 peppercorns
- 1 onion, quartered
- 1 carrot, halved
- chestnut stuffing (see page 69)
- sausage and celery stuffing (see page 69)
- 50g/2oz butter, softened
- 175g/6oz streaky bacon
- about 2 tablespoons flour

*Garnish*

- 450g/1lb pork chipolata sausages
- 225g/8oz streaky bacon
- sprigs watercress

Cover the turkey giblets with water. Add salt, bring to the boil and skim. Add the bay leaf, parsley, peppercorns, onion and carrot. Cover and simmer slowly for about 1 hour. Strain the stock and let it cool. Skim off fat when cold.

Stuff the turkey using chestnut stuffing for the breast cavity and sausage and celery stuffing for the body cavity. Put the turkey in a large roasting pan. Spread the butter over the bird and drape the bacon rashers over the breast and legs. Cover with cooking foil. Roast at 170°C/325°F/gas 3 for 3½ to 4 hours. Towards the end of cooking, remove the foil and rashers and baste well to crispen and brown the skin.

Prepare the garnish. Place the chipolatas in a greased baking tin and cook in the oven for about 20 minutes or until browned. Roll up the bacon rashers and put them on metal skewers. Cook with the sausages for about 15 minutes or until crisp.

Transfer the turkey to a hot serving dish. Drain off fat from roasting pan, sprinkle in flour, cook for 2 to 3 minutes, stirring, then blend in reserved giblet stock to make gravy.

Serve the turkey garnished with watercress, chipolatas and bacon rolls, accompanied by roast potatoes, Brussels sprouts, gravy and bread sauce.

# Duckling in Orange Sauce

*6 portions*

2 ducklings (1.5–2kg/3–4lb each)
75g/3oz butter, softened
salt, pepper
4 large oranges
6 peppercorns
1 bay leaf
sprigs parsley
1 onion, quartered
1 piece carrot
1 piece celery
1 tablespoon flour
3 tablespoons orange jelly marmalade
5 tablespoons sherry
sprigs watercress
orange slices

Set the giblets aside. Place the ducklings on a trivet in a roasting pan, smear each bird with softened butter and sprinkle with salt and pepper. Quarter 2 of the oranges and place 4 quarters inside each bird. Roast the ducklings at 180°C/350°F/gas 4 for $1\frac{1}{4}$ to $1\frac{1}{2}$ hours. Prick the birds after 30 minutes and again after 1 hour, basting them each time.

Meanwhile, put the giblets into a saucepan and cover with water. Add salt, peppercorns, herbs and vegetables. Cover and simmer for about 1 hour. Strain, cool and reserve.

Lift the ducklings and trivet out of the roasting pan. Place the ducklings on a hot dish and keep warm. Grate the rind and squeeze the juice of the remaining oranges. Drain off the fat from the pan juices. Sprinkle the flour over the pan juices and stir together over a low heat. Gradually add the grated orange rind and juice, the marmalade and 100ml/4fl oz of the reserved stock. Bring to the boil, simmer for 3 minutes and add the sherry. Season to taste.

Garnish the ducklings with watercress and orange slices and serve with the sauce, boiled new or roast potatoes and green peas.

# Roast Pheasant

*4–6 portions*

- 1 brace young pheasants, well hung, plucked and drawn
- salt, pepper
- 6 peppercorns
- 1 bay leaf
- 3 sprigs parsley
- 1 onion, quartered
- 1 carrot, sliced
- 100g/4oz butter
- 100g/4oz streaky bacon
- flour
- 50g/2oz fresh breadcrumbs
- sprigs watercress

Cover the pheasant giblets with water, adding salt, peppercorns, herbs and vegetables. Simmer for about 1 hour, strain and reserve.

Put 15g/½oz butter inside each bird and the remainder in a roasting pan. Place the birds in the pan, covering each with 2 rashers of bacon. Roast at 190°C/375°F/gas 5 for 50 to 60 minutes, basting the birds from time to time. Remove the bacon for the last 10 minutes of roasting and sprinkle seasoning and flour over the birds. Finish roasting.

Transfer the pheasants to a hot dish. Pour off the fat from the roasting pan and reserve it. Gradually add the reserved giblet stock to the sediment in the pan, stirring well. Bring to the boil and adjust the seasoning if necessary. Fry the breadcrumbs in the reserved roasting fat. Season with salt. Garnish the birds with watercress and serve with the gravy, fried breadcrumbs, bread sauce, redcurrant jelly, game chips and braised celery.

# Pigeon Pie

*4–6 portions*

3 pigeons
100g/4oz streaky bacon
1 large onion, chopped
75g/3oz sliced mushrooms
2 teaspoons prepared mustard
400ml/$\frac{3}{4}$ pint stock
200g/7oz packet frozen puff pastry, thawed
milk for glazing

Carefully remove the meat from the pigeons, cut the bacon into 1cm/$\frac{1}{2}$ inch strips. Stew the pigeon, bacon and vegetables together with the mustard and stock in a covered saucepan over a low heat for 1 hour. Alternatively, cook in a casserole in the oven at 180°C/350°F/gas 4 for the same length of time. Allow to cool, then place in a pie dish.

Roll out the pastry a little larger all round than the pie dish. Moisten the edge of the dish. Cut off a strip of pastry and place around edge of dish. Moisten the strip. Cover with the remaining pastry. Trim and knock up the edges. Make a hole in the centre of the pastry to allow steam to escape. Decorate with leaves made from pastry scraps. Brush with milk.

Set the pie on a baking sheet and bake at 220°C/425°F/gas 7 for 20 to 25 minutes.

# Jugged Hare

*6–8 portions*

- 1 hare (about 2.5kg/5lb)
- 50g/2oz butter
- 100g/4oz streaky bacon, diced
- 6 baby onions
- 2 shallots, sliced
- 1 sprig each parsley, thyme, marjoram
- 1 bay leaf
- 10 black peppercorns
- 1 blade mace
- 1 tablespoon wine or cider vinegar
- 900ml/$1\frac{1}{2}$ pints hot stock
- 25g/1oz flour
- 5 tablespoons cold stock
- Cumberland sauce (see page 74)
- salt, pepper
- forcemeat balls, fried in oil (see page 70)

Ask the butcher to skin and joint the hare, reserving the blood. Rinse the joints and pat them dry with absorbent paper. Melt the butter in a large flameproof casserole and fry the bacon for 3 minutes. Add the onions and shallots and fry gently for 5 minutes. Add the hare joints and brown them on both sides, about 10 minutes. Tie the herbs, peppercorns and mace in a piece of muslin and add to the casserole with the vinegar and hot stock. Cover with a well-fitting lid and simmer very gently for 1 hour.

Lift out the hare joints and the baby onions, and strain off the cooking liquid. Return the hare joints and baby onions to the casserole. Blend the flour with the cold stock and stir into the strained cooking liquid with the Cumberland sauce. Bring to the boil and simmer for about 3 minutes, stirring constantly. Taste for seasoning. Pour the sauce over the hare.

Cover and simmer very gently for 1 hour further or until tender. Remove from the heat and stir in the reserved blood. Reheat without boiling. Serve with forcemeat balls and redcurrant jelly.

# Savouries & Accompaniments

## Scotch Woodcock

*2 portions*

2 eggs
salt, pepper
2 tablespoons milk
15g/$\frac{1}{2}$oz butter
2 slices buttered toast
50g/2oz canned anchovy fillets, drained
capers

Beat the eggs lightly, add the seasoning, milk and butter. Cook gently in a small heavy saucepan, stirring occasionally. Pile the scrambled eggs on to the buttered toast. Garnish with lattice strips of anchovy fillets and with capers. Serve hot.

# Welsh Rarebit

*4 portions*

Melt the butter in a small heavy saucepan and stir in the flour. Cook for 2 to 3 minutes, stirring well. Add the milk and continue stirring until the mixture forms a thick smooth sauce. Then add the beer, if used, the mustard, Worcestershire sauce, cheese and seasoning to taste. Heat gently but avoid overcooking.

Spread the mixture over slices of buttered toast and brown under a hot grill. Garnish with parsley or tomato and serve at once.

25g/1oz butter
1 tablespoon flour
5 tablespoons milk, or 3 tablespoons milk and 2 tablespoons beer
1 teaspoon prepared mustard
few drops Worcestershire sauce
about 150g/5oz grated cheese (preferably Lancashire)
salt, pepper
4 slices buttered toast
4 sprigs parsley or 4 slices tomato

# Mushrooms on Toast

*4 portions*

Heat the butter in a frying pan. Add the mushrooms and a little seasoning and fry gently until cooked. Mix the mustard with the sherry and add to the prepared white sauce, then add the mushrooms.

Pile the mushrooms and sauce on to the buttered toast. Garnish with chopped parsley and a little cayenne or paprika. Serve hot.

25g/1oz butter
225g/8oz sliced mushrooms
salt, pepper
1 teaspoon dry mustard
2 tablespoons sherry
300ml/$\frac{1}{2}$ pint white sauce (see page 72)
4 slices buttered toast
2 tablespoons chopped parsley
cayenne or paprika pepper

# Potted Cheese

100g/4oz butter
225g/8oz grated cheese
3 tablespoons sherry
1 teaspoon dry mustard
salt, pepper

*Seal*
50–75g/2–3oz butter, melted

Beat the butter until creamy. Add the grated cheese and mix well. Stir in the sherry and mustard. Check the seasoning and adjust if necessary. Beat until smooth. Store the cheese in small pâté dishes or earthenware pots. Pour melted butter on top of each container, to seal. Chill, cover and store in a cool place or in the refrigerator. Serve chilled with toast.

# Sage and Onion Stuffing

*4–6 portions*

450g/1lb onions, quartered
10 fresh sage leaves or 1 teaspoon crushed dried sage
100g/4oz fresh breadcrumbs
40g/1½oz butter, melted
1 egg yolk
2 tablespoons chopped parsley
salt, pepper

Put the onions into boiling salted water and parboil for 10 to 15 minutes. If using fresh sage, add the leaves just 30 seconds before draining the onions. Chop the onion and sage leaves very finely. If using dried sage, add to the chopped onions. Add the breadcrumbs, butter, egg yolk, parsley and seasoning. Use for stuffing goose, duck and pork.

# Chestnut Stuffing

*6–8 portions*

Cut the tops from the chestnuts. Roast the nuts in the oven for 20 minutes at 180°C/350°F/gas 4 or boil them in water for 10 to 15 minutes. Remove the outer and inner skins, put the nuts in a pan with the milk or stock. Simmer gently until tender. Rub through a sieve, add the butter, sugar and seasoning. Use for stuffing breast cavity of turkey.

1kg/2lb chestnuts
300ml/½ pint milk or stock
50g/2oz butter
¼ teaspoon sugar
salt, pepper

# Sausage and Celery Stuffing

*6–8 portions*

Melt the butter and gently fry the onion and celery for about 5 minutes. Mix all the ingredients together thoroughly. Use for stuffing body cavity of turkey.

25g/1oz butter
1 onion, chopped
2 sticks celery, chopped
350g/12oz sausagemeat
100g/4oz fresh breadcrumbs
grated rind and juice 1 lemon
3 tablespoons chopped parsley
1 teaspoon dried thyme
1 teaspoon salt
¼ teaspoon black pepper
1 small egg, beaten

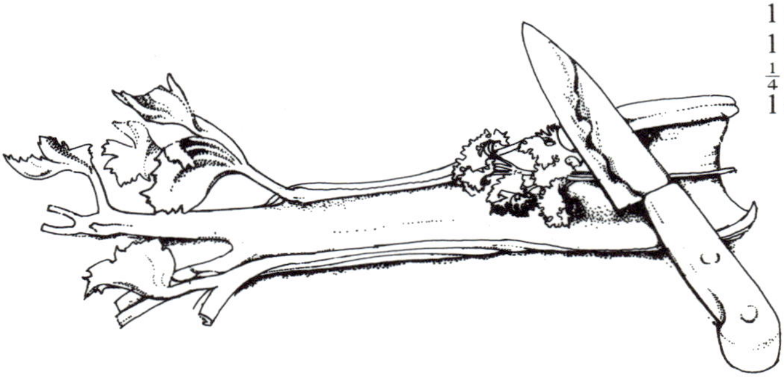

# Forcemeat

*4–6 portions*

100g/4oz fresh breadcrumbs
50g/2oz shredded suet
50g/2oz chopped ham or lean bacon (optional)
1 tablespoon chopped parsley
½ teaspoon dried mixed herbs
pinch each ground mace, grated nutmeg
finely grated rind 1 lemon
salt, pepper
1 teaspoon dry mustard
1 egg, beaten
milk for mixing (optional)

Mix all the ingredients together in a bowl adding milk if necessary to moisten the forcemeat. Use for stuffing veal or poultry or shape the mixture into small balls, roll them in flour and fry them in oil to use as a garnish for stews and jugged hare.

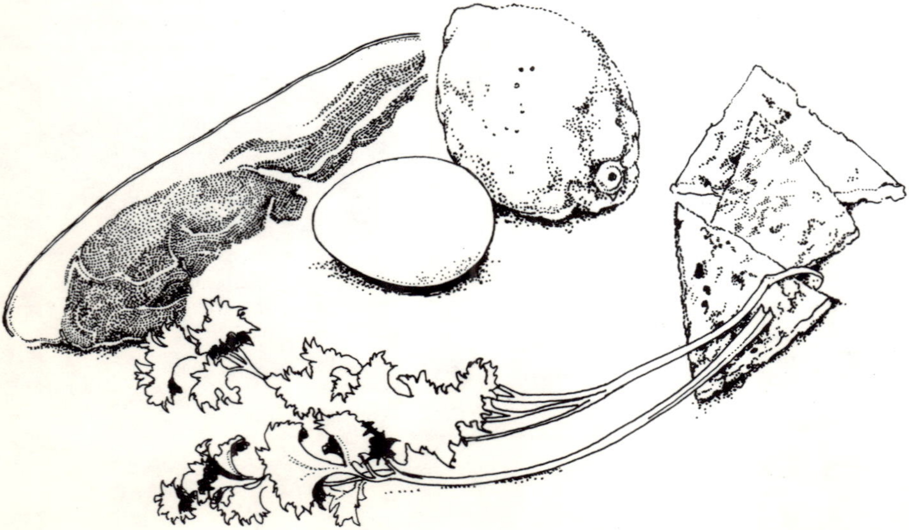

# Mustard Dumplings

*6 portions*

Sift the flour, mustard and salt into a basin. Rub in the butter. Add sufficient milk to make a soft, but not wet dough. Using floured hands, shape the mixture into 6 or 12 balls. Cook the dumplings in the gravy of a meat casserole during the last 20 to 30 minutes of cooking, at 180°C/350°F/gas 4. Sprinkle the tops of the dumplings with paprika before serving with the casserole.

250g/9oz self-raising flour
$1\frac{1}{2}$ teaspoons dry mustard
$\frac{1}{4}$ teaspoon salt
75g/3oz butter
about 150ml/$\frac{1}{4}$ pint milk
paprika pepper

# Mustard Croûtons

*4 portions*

Put the bread triangles or cubes into a shallow bowl. Sift the mustard over them through a fine sieve and shake the bowl gently to coat the bread. Fry in hot oil until golden brown. Drain well on absorbent paper. Sprinkle with salt and serve as a garnish to soups and stews.

2 large slices white bread, cut into small triangles or cubes
1 teaspoon dry mustard
oil for frying
salt

# Sauces, Dressings & Butters

## White Sauce

50g/2oz butter
50g/2oz flour
$\frac{1}{4}$ teaspoon salt
white pepper
600ml/1 pint milk

Melt the butter in a saucepan and stir in the flour. Cook for 2 to 3 minutes without colouring. Add the seasonings. Draw the pan from the heat and slowly add the milk, stirring constantly. Return to the heat and bring to the boil, still stirring. Simmer for about 3 minutes. Adjust the seasoning.

*Notes:* 1. To make a thinner pouring sauce, use half the quantity of fat and flour to the same volume of liquid.

2. To make a richer version, the sauce may be finished with cream and egg yolk(s).

3. White sauce may be flavoured in many different ways, using various herbs and spices, lemon juice and white wine, or by substituting a white stock from veal, chicken, fish or vegetables. Grated cheese or sautéd mushrooms may be added to the basic white sauce.

# Mustard Sauce

Fry the onion in the butter until softened. Sprinkle with the flour and cook for 2 to 3 minutes. Add the liquid gradually, stirring all the time, and bring to the boil. Add the mustard mixed with the vinegar. Simmer for 2 to 3 minutes. Season to taste.

1 small onion or shallot, finely chopped
25g/1oz butter
25g/1oz flour
300ml/$\frac{1}{2}$ pint fish stock, or milk and water
2 teaspoons dry mustard
1–2 tablespoons vinegar
salt, pepper

# Bread Sauce

Stick the onion with the cloves. Place in a pan with the milk and bring slowly to the boil. Remove from the heat. Stir in the rest of the ingredients. Leave in a warm place for about 2 hours. Remove the onion and reheat the sauce gently, adding a little more milk if required.

1 small onion
5 or 6 cloves
600ml/1 pint milk
25g/1oz butter
175g/6oz fresh breadcrumbs
pinch ground mace
salt, white pepper

# Cumberland Sauce

grated rind and juice 1 large orange
225g/8oz redcurrant jelly
$1\frac{1}{2}$ teaspoons dry mustard
1 teaspoon Worcestershire sauce
juice $\frac{1}{2}$ lemon
pinch powdered ginger
small pinch cayenne pepper (optional)
4 tablespoons port

Put all the ingredients, except the port, into a small pan and leave over a low heat until all the jelly has dissolved. Stir in the port and cool before serving. Serve with ham, pork, lamb and game.

# Horseradish Sauce

150ml/$\frac{1}{4}$ pint double cream
25g/1oz horseradish, peeled and grated
1 tablespoon cider vinegar
1–2 teaspoons castor sugar
salt, pepper, prepared mustard

Whip the cream lightly. Fold the horseradish into the cream and add the vinegar, sugar and seasonings to taste. Serve with boiled fish, beef or tongue, or with mild, smooth cheeses such as Edam, Gouda or Jarlsberg.

# Piquant Sauce

20g/$\frac{3}{4}$oz butter
2 tablespoons flour
300ml/$\frac{1}{2}$ pint beef stock
1 tablespoon prepared mustard
1 tablespoon horseradish sauce
salt, pepper

Melt the butter over a low heat, add the flour and cook for 2 to 3 minutes. Remove from the heat. Slowly blend in the stock. Return to the heat and bring to the boil, stirring all the time. Boil for 2 minutes. Stir in the mustard and horseradish sauce and season to taste. Serve with beef.

COLMAN'S
MUSTARD

# Mayonnaise

Put egg yolks, seasonings and sugar into a basin. Mix thoroughly, then add the oil drop by drop, beating well with a whisk the whole time, until thick and smooth. Beat in the lemon juice and vinegar.

For a thinner mix, add a little cream or top of the milk. Should the sauce curdle, take a fresh egg yolk and begin again adding the curdled mayonnaise very slowly in the same way as the oil is added to the original egg yolks. This mayonnaise will keep well for a month in an airtight plastic container or jar in a refrigerator.

2 large egg yolks
1 teaspoon dry mustard
$\frac{1}{2}$ teaspoon salt
$\frac{1}{8}$ teaspoon pepper
1 teaspoon castor sugar
300ml/$\frac{1}{2}$ pint oil
1 tablespoon lemon juice
1 tablespoon wine or distilled malt vinegar
cream or top of the milk (optional)

# Mustard Dressing (1)

Add the oil to the mustard, a little at a time, beating until all the lumps have been dispersed. Add the lemon juice and mix thoroughly. Use as a salad dressing.

$2\frac{1}{2}$ tablespoons vegetable oil
$2\frac{1}{2}$ teaspoons dry mustard
juice $\frac{1}{2}$ lemon

# Mustard Dressing (2)

Shake or whisk together the vinegar, oil, seasoning and sugar if used. Add the mustard and mix well. Taste for seasoning. Serve with fish and salads.

1 tablespoon vinegar
3 tablespoons oil
salt, pepper
1 teaspoon sugar (optional)
2–3 tablespoons prepared mustard

*Previous page: Mushrooms on toast (recipe page 67).*
*Opposite: Queen of puddings (recipe page 81).*

# Cheese Butter

100g/4oz butter, softened
50g/2oz grated cheese
1 teaspoon dry mustard
1 teaspoon Worcestershire sauce

Cream together the ingredients until they are well blended. Use as a spread with hot crusty loaves for serving with soups, stews, salads and grilled dishes.

# Mustard Butter

100g/4oz butter, softened
2–3 tablespoons prepared mustard

Mix the butter with the mustard. Cream until smooth. Use as a sandwich spread with ham, tongue or fish fillings, also with stuffed eggs, boiled vegetables, fish dishes and with grilled or fried steaks.

# Brandy Butter

75g/3oz unsalted butter
75g/3oz castor sugar
grated rind $\frac{1}{2}$ orange
2–3 teaspoons lemon juice
5 tablespoons brandy

Cream the butter thoroughly, then gradually beat in the sugar, grated orange rind and lemon juice. Finally beat in the brandy. Transfer the brandy butter to a bowl. Cover tightly with foil or cling-film and chill before serving with Christmas pudding and mince pies.

# Puddings

## Apple Pie with Quince

*4–6 portions*

750g/1½lb cooking apples, peeled, cored and sliced
2 ripe quinces, peeled, cored and chopped
75–100g/3–4oz sugar
2 tablespoons water
shortcrust pastry, using 175g/6oz flour etc (see page 15)
castor sugar

Mix the apples and quinces and place in layers in a 1 litre/1¾ pint pie dish, sprinkling each layer (except the top one) with sugar and water. Pile up the fruit in the centre of the dish in a dome shape or use a pie funnel to support the pastry.

Roll out the pastry a little larger all round than the pie dish. Moisten the edge of the dish. Cut off a strip of pastry and place around edge of dish. Moisten the strip. Cover with the remaining pastry. Trim and knock up the edges. Make a hole in the centre of the pastry to allow steam to escape. Decorate with leaves made from pastry scraps. Brush with water.

Set the pie on a baking sheet and bake at 200°C/400°F/gas 6 for about 40 minutes. Test the fruit with a skewer to check that it is tender. The pastry should be crisp and golden brown. Dredge the pie with castor sugar and serve hot or cold.

# Eve's Pudding

*3–4 portions*

350g/12oz cooking apples, peeled, cored and thinly sliced
100g/4oz castor sugar
50g/2oz butter
1 egg, lightly beaten
75g/3oz self-raising flour
milk

Place half the apple slices in a buttered 900ml/1½ pint pie dish. Sprinkle with half the sugar then cover with the rest of the apple slices. Cream the butter with the remaining sugar. Add the egg a little at a time, then the sifted flour and enough milk to give the mixture a soft dropping consistency. Cover the apples with the mixture. Bake at 180°C/350°F/gas 4 for about 1 hour. Sprinkle with castor sugar and serve hot, with cream or custard.

# Baked Apples

*4 portions*

4 large cooking apples, cored
50g/2oz mixed dried fruit
25g/1oz soft brown sugar
4 tablespoons golden syrup
25g/1oz butter

Slit the skins in a ring half-way down the apple, using a vegetable knife. Place the apples in a shallow ovenproof dish, containing 5mm/¼ inch water. Mix the dried fruit with the sugar and pack the mixture into the core cavities. Pour 1 tablespoon syrup over each apple and dot with butter. Bake at 200°C/400°F/gas 6 for about 40 minutes, until tender. Serve hot, with cream or custard.

# Rhubarb Crumble

*4–6 portions*

Cut the rhubarb into 2.5cm/1 inch pieces. Rub the butter into the flour until the mixture resembles fine breadcrumbs. Stir in half the sugar. Place the rhubarb in a buttered 900ml/1½ pint pie dish and sprinkle each layer with the remaining sugar and the water. Cover the fruit with the crumble mixture and bake at 180°C/350°F/gas 4 for 40 to 50 minutes until the fruit is cooked and the crumble golden brown.

750g/1½lb rhubarb, trimmed
75g/3oz butter
175g/6oz flour
175g/6oz castor sugar
2 tablespoons water

# Queen of Puddings

*4–6 portions*

Put the breadcrumbs, 2 tablespoons of the sugar and the lemon rind into a large bowl. Heat the milk with the butter and pour over the breadcrumb mixture. Leave to stand for about 30 minutes so that the crumbs swell. Beat the egg yolks and stir them into the crumb mixture. Pour into a buttered 900ml/1½ pint pie dish and bake at 200°C/400°F/gas 6 for 30 minutes, spreading the top with jam after the first 20 minutes.

Whisk the egg whites stiffly, beat in half the remaining sugar a little at a time. Fold in the rest of the sugar and pile the meringue on top of the pudding. Bake at 180°C/350°F/gas 4 until the meringue is lightly browned.

175g/6oz fresh breadcrumbs
150g/5oz castor sugar
grated rind 1 lemon
600ml/1 pint milk
50g/2oz butter
3 eggs, separated
6 tablespoons jam

# Canary Pudding

*4 portions*

100g/4oz self-raising flour
100g/4oz butter
100g/4oz castor sugar
2 eggs, beaten
grated rind and juice 1 lemon
4 tablespoons apricot jam

Butter a 900ml/1½ pint pudding basin. Sift the flour. Cream the butter and sugar until light and fluffy. Beat in the eggs a little at a time. Add half the grated lemon rind. Fold in the flour. Turn the mixture into the prepared basin. Cover with greased greaseproof paper and foil and steam for 1½ hours. Prepare a sauce by heating the rest of the lemon rind and the lemon juice with the apricot jam. Remove the foil and paper from the pudding and turn out on to a hot dish. Pour the sauce over and serve.

*Note:* The same sponge mixture may be steamed in individual buttered dariole moulds and served with the jam sauce. They are known as Castle Puddings.

# Christmas Pudding

*8 portions*

100g/4oz flour
1 teaspoon mixed spice
1 teaspoon cinnamon
100g/4oz fresh breadcrumbs
100g/4oz shredded suet
100g/4oz demerara sugar
350g/12oz mixed dried fruit
50g/2oz mixed chopped peel
finely grated rind 1 large orange
50g/2oz chopped almonds
3 eggs, beaten
1 tablespoon black treacle
1 tablespoon brandy
about 4 tablespoons brown ale
brandy butter (see page 78)

Grease a 900ml/1½ pint pudding basin. Sift the flour and spices into a mixing bowl, add the remaining dry ingredients and mix together thoroughly. Add the eggs, treacle, brandy and ale and mix to a fairly soft consistency. Turn into the prepared basin. Cover with greased greaseproof paper and foil and steam for 5 hours. Allow to cool. Remove foil and paper and cover with fresh paper and foil. Store in a dry, airy place. To reheat, steam for 1½ hours. Serve with brandy butter.

# Mince Pies

*20 pies*

Grease 20 tartlet tins. Divide the pastry into 2 equal portions. Roll out one piece 3mm/⅛ inch thick and cut into 20 rounds with a 7.5cm/3 inch cutter. Line the tartlet tins with the pastry rounds. Fill each tartlet with mincemeat. Damp the edges of the pastry. Roll out the rest of the pastry, cut out lids with a 7cm/2½ inch cutter and use to cover the pies. Make a tiny slit in the top of each, using a sharp-pointed knife.

Brush the pies with milk and bake at 220°C/425°F/gas 7 for about 20 minutes. Turn the pies out of the tins and cool on a wire rack. Dust with sifted icing sugar.

- shortcrust pastry, using 450g/1lb flour etc (see page 15)
- 450g/1lb mincemeat (see below)
- milk for glazing
- icing sugar

# Mincemeat

Put the raisins, mixed peel, half the sultanas and currants and the apples twice through a mincer. Add the rest of the dried fruit, the suet, sugar, citrus rinds and juices, mixed spice, nutmeg and brandy or rum. Mix well and keep covered in a bowl. Stir each day for 1 week. Turn into clean, dry jars, leaving a 2.5cm/1 inch space at the top. Cover with waxed paper and cling-film. Allow the mincemeat to mature for several weeks before use.

- 750g/1½lb raisins
- 450g/1lb mixed peel
- 450g/1lb sultanas
- 450g/1lb currants
- 1kg/2lb apples, peeled and cored
- 450g/1lb shredded suet
- 750g/1½lb soft brown sugar
- rind and juice 1 lemon
- rind and juice 1 orange
- 1½ tablespoons mixed spice
- ½ nutmeg, grated
- 300ml/½ pint brandy or rum

# Pancakes

*4 portions*

100g/4oz flour
$\frac{1}{4}$ teaspoon salt
1 egg
300ml/$\frac{1}{2}$ pint milk
oil for frying

Sift together the flour and salt. Add the egg, then gradually beat in half the milk to make a smooth batter. Beat in the remaining milk and pour the batter into a jug. Leave to stand for 30 minutes.

Lightly grease an 18cm/7 inch frying pan and heat until hot. Quickly pour in enough batter to coat the bottom of the pan thinly, tilting the pan so that the bottom is evenly covered. Cook until the underside is golden brown, turn and cook on the other side. Slip out on to a warm plate, cover and keep hot. Repeat until all the batter is used.

# Bakewell Tart

*4 portions*

shortcrust pastry, using 100g/4oz flour etc (see page 15)
50g/2oz butter
50g/2oz castor sugar
1 egg, lightly beaten
50g/2oz flour
25g/1oz fresh breadcrumbs
few drops almond essence
raspberry jam
icing sugar

Line an 18cm/7 inch pie plate or flan ring with pastry. Cream the butter and sugar, beat in the egg a little at a time. Then add the flour, breadcrumbs and almond essence. Spread the pastry with a good layer of jam, then put the sponge mixture on top. Bake at 200°C/400°F/gas 6 for 30 minutes. Sprinkle with sifted icing sugar. Serve hot or cold.

# Dorset Treacle Tart

*4–6 portions*

Line a 20cm/8 inch pie plate or flan tin with the pastry. Roll out the trimmings and cut into four 25cm/10 inch long strips. Mix together the remaining ingredients and spread inside the pastry case. Twist the pastry strips and dampen the ends. Place across the tart in a star design. Bake at 200°C/400°F/gas 6 for 30 to 35 minutes until the pastry is golden brown. Serve hot or cold, with cream.

- shortcrust pastry, using 175g/6oz flour etc (see page 15)
- 5 tablespoons golden syrup
- 1 tablespoon black treacle
- 50g/2oz fresh white breadcrumbs
- 1 cooking apple, peeled, cored and chopped
- 50g/2oz mixed dried fruit

# Meringues

*6 portions*

Prepare baking sheets by lining with lightly oiled greaseproof paper. Thoroughly clean the bowl and whisk used for whisking the egg whites to ensure that they are grease-free. Put the egg whites into the bowl. Whisk them until they are stiff and dry. Whisk in the granulated sugar until the mixture is stiff. Fold in the castor sugar with a metal tablespoon. Use a piping bag with a rose tube and pipe out 12 shells spaced 1cm/$\frac{1}{2}$ inch apart on the prepared baking sheets.

Place in the oven at 110°C/225°F/gas $\frac{1}{4}$ for 3 to 4 hours. Remove from the baking sheets while still warm. Cool on wire racks. Sandwich the meringues together with whipped cream before serving.

- 2 egg whites
- 50g/2oz granulated sugar
- 50g/2oz castor sugar
- 300ml/$\frac{1}{2}$ pint double cream, whipped

# Summer Pudding

*4–6 portions*

1 large white loaf (2 or 3 days old), thinly sliced
750g/1½lb mixed soft fruit (raspberries, redcurrants, strawberries, etc)
about 100g/4oz castor sugar or 5 tablespoons honey

Remove the crusts from the bread. Line a 1 litre/1¾ pint pudding basin with bread slices, cutting them into smaller pieces if necessary. Stew the fruit in a very little water until soft, adding sugar or honey to taste. Half-fill the lined basin with fruit, cover with bread, then add the rest of the fruit. Cover the top of the basin with more bread, fitting closely.

Cover with a plate that fits inside the basin on top of the bread lid. Place a heavy weight on top of the plate. Chill in the refrigerator overnight or longer. Turn out carefully and serve with whipped cream.

# Trifle

*4 portions*

4 individual sponge cakes
raspberry jam
150ml/¼ pint sherry
2 tablespoons brandy (optional)
finely grated rind 1 lemon
25g/1oz chopped almonds
600ml/1 pint custard (see right)
300ml/½ pint double cream
1 tablespoon castor sugar
glacé cherries
angelica or flaked almonds

Split the sponge cakes in 2 and spread with jam. Sandwich the cakes together again and arrange them in a deep glass dish. Pour the sherry and brandy, if used, over the cakes and sprinkle with grated lemon rind and chopped almonds. Cover with custard. Whip the cream and sugar together and pile on top of the trifle. Decorate with glacé cherries and angelica or flaked almonds.

# Rhubarb Fool

*6 portions*

Put the rhubarb in a heavy stainless steel saucepan. Add the sugar and water and simmer gently until the rhubarb is tender. Drain most of the syrup from the stewed rhubarb and purée the fruit using a sieve or an electric blender. Mix the purée with the custard. Whip the cream lightly and add to the purée and custard mixture. Chill and serve with sponge fingers.

450g/1lb rhubarb, trimmed and diced
100g/4oz sugar
150ml/$\frac{1}{4}$ pint water
300ml/$\frac{1}{2}$ pint custard (see below)
300ml/$\frac{1}{2}$ pint double cream

# Custard

Warm the milk. Beat the egg, egg yolk and sugar together in a bowl and pour in the milk. Strain into a pan and cook very gently until thickened, stirring constantly with a wooden spoon.
*Note:* The use of a double saucepan is preferable for making this sauce.

300ml/$\frac{1}{2}$ pint milk
1 egg
1 egg yolk
1 tablespoon castor sugar (preferably vanilla-flavoured)

# Fresh Fruit Salad

*4 portions*

1 tablespoon lemon juice
4 tablespoons orange juice
2 tablespoons liquid honey
3 teaspoons Cointreau (optional)
1 large banana, sliced
100g/4oz grapes
1 apple, cored and sliced
2 oranges, divided into segments, pith cut away and pips removed
2 slices pineapple, skin, eyes and inner core cut away, flesh cut into small pieces
1 piece melon, peeled and seeded, scooped into balls

Mix the lemon and orange juices with the honey and Cointreau if used. Put the fruits in a glass bowl and mix them gently with a fork and tablespoon. Pour the sweetened juice over the fruit and chill. Serve with whipped cream. The content of the fruit salad may be varied according to seasonal availability. In summer, soft fruits and peaches may be included.

# Syllabub

*6 portions*

finely grated rind and juice 1 large lemon
150ml/$\frac{1}{4}$ pint medium-sweet sherry
50g/2oz castor sugar
2 tablespoons brandy
300ml/$\frac{1}{2}$ pint double cream

Put the lemon rind and juice, sherry, sugar and brandy into a bowl. Stir until the sugar dissolves. Add the cream and whisk until thick and foamy. Spoon into serving glasses, cover with cling-film and chill.

# Bakes

## Sally Lunns

*2 cakes*

15g/½oz fresh yeast or 2 teaspoons dried yeast
1 teaspoon sugar
300ml/½ pint warm milk
450g/1lb strong plain flour
1 teaspoon salt
2 eggs, beaten
50g/2oz butter, melted and cooled

*Glaze*
2 tablespoons water
2 tablespoons sugar

Stir the fresh or dried yeast and the sugar into the warm milk. If using dried yeast, allow to stand for about 10 minutes until frothy. Mix in one quarter of the flour and leave in a warm place for about 20 minutes until the yeast batter is foamy.

Mix the rest of the flour with the salt and stir into the yeast batter with the eggs and melted butter. Beat until a smooth batter is formed. Pour into 2 lightly greased 15cm/6 inch cake tins. Place the tins in lightly oiled polythene bags and leave at room temperature until double in size, about 1½ hours.

Bake at 220°C/425°F/gas 7 for about 20 minutes until golden brown. Transfer the cakes to a wire rack. To make the glaze, boil the water and sugar. Brush the hot cakes with glaze, then leave to cool slightly. Slice each cake into two or three layers and serve warm with clotted cream or butter.

# Chelsea Buns

*9 buns*

15g/½oz fresh yeast or 2 teaspoons dried yeast
½ teaspoon sugar
80ml/3fl oz warm milk
225g/8oz strong plain flour
½ teaspoon salt
25g/1oz margarine
1 egg, beaten
25g/1oz butter, melted
75g/3oz currants or sultanas
25g/1oz mixed peel
50g/2oz soft brown sugar
warm honey or golden syrup

Stir the fresh or dried yeast and the sugar into the warm milk. If using dried yeast, allow to stand for about 10 minutes until frothy. Mix in one quarter of the flour and leave in a warm place for about 20 minutes until the yeast batter is foamy.

Mix the rest of the flour with the salt. Rub in the margarine. Stir the flour mixture and the egg into the yeast batter and mix to a soft dough. Turn on to a lightly floured board and knead until smooth. Place the dough in a lightly oiled polythene bag and leave at room temperature until double in size, about 1½ hours.

Roll out to a rectangle 30 × 23cm/12 × 9 inches. Brush the dough with melted butter and sprinkle the dried fruit, mixed peel and brown sugar on top. Roll up the dough like a Swiss roll, starting from the longer side. Cut into 9 equal slices and place close together, cut side down, in a greased 18cm/7 inch square baking tin. Cover and leave in a warm place for about 40 minutes until the buns have doubled in size and have joined together.

Bake at 220°C/425°F/gas 7 for about 25 minutes until golden brown. Transfer the buns to a wire rack and brush with warm honey or syrup while they are still hot. Break the buns apart when cool.

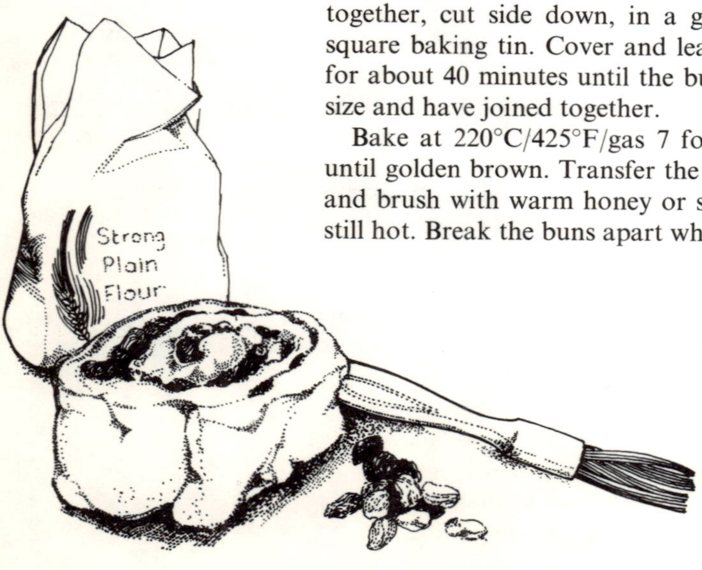

# Hot Cross Buns

*12 buns*

Mix the warm milk and water. Stir in the fresh yeast, or the dried yeast and 1 teaspoon sugar. If using dried yeast, allow to stand for about 10 minutes until frothy. Mix in one quarter of the flour and leave in a warm place for about 20 minutes until the yeast batter is foamy.

Mix the rest of the flour with the sugar and remaining ingredients, stir into the yeast batter and mix to a soft dough. Turn on to a lightly floured board and knead until smooth. Place the dough in a lightly oiled polythene bag and leave at room temperature until double in size, about 1½ hours.

Divide the dough into 12 pieces and shape into buns. Arrange the buns, well spaced, on a floured baking sheet. Cover with lightly oiled polythene and allow to rise at room temperature for about 40 minutes.

Use strips of leftover pastry to make crosses or pipe on crosses made from a paste of 2 tablespoons each flour and water. Alternatively, slash the dough with a very sharp knife to make a cross. Bake at 220°C/425°F/gas 7 for 15 to 20 minutes until golden brown. Transfer the buns to a wire rack. To make the glaze, boil the milk, water and sugar. Brush the hot buns twice with glaze, then leave to cool.

150ml/¼ pint warm milk
80ml/3fl oz warm water
25g/1oz fresh yeast or 1 tablespoon dried yeast
50g/2oz sugar
450g/1lb strong plain flour
1 teaspoon salt
1½ teaspoons mixed spice
½ teaspoon ground cinnamon
½ teaspoon grated nutmeg
50g/2oz butter, melted and cooled
1 egg, beaten
100g/4oz currants
50g/2oz mixed peel

*Glaze*
2 tablespoons milk
2 tablespoons water
40g/1½oz sugar

# Teacakes

*5 teacakes*

- 15g/$\frac{1}{2}$oz fresh yeast or 2 teaspoons dried yeast
- 25g/1oz sugar
- 300ml/$\frac{1}{2}$ pint warm milk
- 450g/1lb strong plain flour
- 1 teaspoon salt
- 25g/1oz lard
- 50g/2oz currants
- milk for glazing

Stir the fresh yeast, or the dried yeast and 1 teaspoon sugar, into the warm milk. If using dried yeast, allow to stand for about 10 minutes until frothy. Mix the sugar, flour and salt, and rub in the lard. Stir the flour mixture and currants into the yeast batter and mix to a soft dough. Turn on to a lightly floured board and knead until smooth. Place the dough in a lightly oiled polythene bag and leave at room temperature until double in size, about 1$\frac{1}{2}$ hours.

Divide the dough into 5 pieces and shape into rounds. Roll out each round to about 13cm/5 inches across and 1cm/$\frac{1}{2}$ inch thick. Place well apart on a greased baking sheet. Cover with lightly oiled polythene and allow to rise at room temperature for about 40 minutes.

Brush the tops with milk and bake at 220°C/425°F/gas 7 for about 20 minutes until golden brown. Cool on a wire rack. Split in 2, toast, spread with butter and serve hot.

# Irish Soda Bread

- 450g/1lb flour (white, or white and wholemeal)
- 1 teaspoon salt
- 2 teaspoons bicarbonate of soda
- 1 tablespoon cream of tartar
- 25g/1oz lard
- about 300ml/$\frac{1}{2}$ pint milk

Sift the flour, salt, bicarbonate of soda and cream of tartar into a bowl. Rub in the lard and add enough milk to make a soft dough. Turn the mixture on to a floured board and knead lightly for 1 minute. Shape into a round and place on a greased baking sheet. Mark with a cross, cutting deeply—almost to the base of the dough.

Bake at 220°C/425°F/gas 7 for 40 to 50 minutes

until well risen, lightly browned and firm underneath. Turn out and cool on a wire rack.
*Note:* If sour milk or buttermilk are used, reduce the quantity of cream of tartar by half.

# Cornish Scones

*12 scones*

225g/8oz self-raising flour
½ teaspoon salt
50g/2oz butter or margarine
25g/1oz castor sugar
about 150ml/¼ pint milk
milk for glazing

Sift together the flour and salt. Rub in the fat and add the sugar. Mix to a soft dough with milk. Roll out the dough on a lightly floured board to 1cm/½ inch thickness and cut into rounds with a 4cm/1½ inch cutter. Place on greased baking sheets and brush with milk. Bake at 220°C/425°F/gas 7 for about 10 minutes. Cool on a wire rack. Serve the scones with jam and clotted cream.

# Cheese Scones

*12 scones*

225g/8oz self-raising flour
½ teaspoon dry mustard
½ teaspoon salt
50g/2oz butter or margarine
40g/1½oz grated cheese
about 150ml/¼ pint milk
1 egg, beaten

Sift together the flour, mustard and salt. Rub in the fat until the mixture resembles fine breadcrumbs. Add the cheese and mix to a soft dough with milk. Roll out the dough on a lightly floured board to 1cm/½ inch thickness and cut into rounds with a 4cm/1½ inch cutter. Place on greased baking sheets and brush with beaten egg. Bake at 220°C/425°F/gas 7 for about 10 minutes. Cool on a wire rack. Serve with butter.

# Savoury Girdle Scones

*12 scones*

225g/8oz self-raising flour
$\frac{1}{2}$ teaspoon salt
$\frac{1}{2}$ teaspoon dry mustard
50g/2oz margarine and/or lard
1 tablespoon finely chopped parsley
$\frac{1}{2}$ teaspoon dried mixed herbs
50g/2oz streaky bacon, chopped and fried
about 80ml/3fl oz milk

Sift the flour, salt and mustard into a mixing bowl. Rub in the fat until the mixture resembles fine breadcrumbs. Stir in the parsley, mixed herbs and bacon and mix to a soft dough with milk. Turn the dough on to a lightly floured board, divide it in half and roll out into 2 rounds about 5mm/$\frac{1}{4}$ inch thick. Cut each round into 6 even triangles.

Brush off surplus flour and place the scones, four at a time, on a hot, greased girdle for 3 to 4 minutes on each side. Turn the scones with a palette knife when browned on the first side. Fold in a clean tea towel until all are cooked. Serve warm with butter.

# Drop Scones

*12 scones*

225g/8oz self-raising flour
$\frac{1}{2}$ teaspoon salt
1–2 tablespoons sugar
1 egg, beaten
15g/$\frac{1}{2}$oz butter, melted
about 100ml/4fl oz milk

Sift together the flour and salt. Add the sugar, beaten egg, butter and enough milk to give a stiff batter. Heat a girdle and lightly grease it with oil or melted fat. Drop spoonfuls of the batter on to the girdle and cook for 2 or 3 minutes, then turn with a palette knife and cook on the other side. Place the drop scones inside a clean tea towel until all are cooked. Serve fresh with butter.

# Victoria Sandwich Cake

100g/4oz butter or margarine
100g/4oz castor sugar
2 large eggs
100g/4oz self-raising flour, sieved
2 tablespoons raspberry jam
icing or castor sugar

Grease two 18cm/7 inch sandwich tins and line with greased greaseproof paper. Cream the butter or margarine with the sugar until light and fluffy. Beat in the eggs, one at a time, adding a little of the flour with the second egg to prevent the mixture from curdling. Fold in the rest of the flour lightly but briskly, using a metal tablespoon. Turn the mixture into the prepared tins and smooth the tops with a spatula.

Bake at 180°C/350°F/gas 4 for 25 to 35 minutes. Test while the cakes are still in the oven by pressing the centre of the surface lightly with the finger. The cake will feel firm if it is cooked. If it feels soft, allow longer cooking. Turn out the cakes on to a wire rack to cool. Sandwich the two halves together with jam. Dredge the top with icing or castor sugar.

# Date and Walnut Loaf

225g/8oz self-raising flour
$\frac{1}{4}$ teaspoon salt
$\frac{1}{4}$ teaspoon mixed spice
2 tablespoons sugar
25g/1oz chopped walnuts
75g/3oz chopped dates
2 tablespoons golden syrup
5 tablespoons milk
2 tablespoons malt extract

Grease a 450g/1lb loaf tin. Sift together the flour, salt and spice. Add the sugar, chopped walnuts and dates. Heat the syrup, milk and malt extract over a gentle heat in a heavy saucepan until warm and blended. Add to the dry ingredients and beat well.

Turn into the loaf tin and bake at 180°C/350°F/gas 4 for 1 hour. Turn out and cool on a wire rack. Serve cold, sliced with butter.

# Cut-and-come-again Cake

225g/8oz self-raising flour
$\frac{1}{4}$ teaspoon salt
1 teaspoon mixed spice
100g/4oz butter or margarine
100g/4oz castor sugar
250g/9oz mixed dried fruit
1 teaspoon grated orange or lemon rind
1 egg
about 100ml/4fl oz milk and water

Line and grease a 15cm/6 inch cake tin. Sift together the flour, salt and spice. Divide the fat into small pieces and rub it into the dry ingredients until the mixture resembles fine breadcrumbs. Stir in the sugar, dried fruit and orange or lemon rind. Make a well in the centre of the mixture and add the egg and milk and water. Mix, beating well.

Turn the mixture into the cake tin and bake at 180°C/350°F/gas 4 for 1 hour 20 minutes. Turn out and cool on a wire rack.

# Seed Cake

Grease and flour a 20cm/8 inch cake tin. Sift together the flour and baking powder. Cream together the fat and sugar. Add the eggs a little at a time. Start to fold in the flour when almost all the eggs have been added, then finally add the caraway seeds. Turn the mixture into the prepared tin and bake at 180°C/350°F/gas 4 for 1 hour. Turn out and cool on a wire rack.

- 225g/8oz flour
- $\frac{1}{4}$ teaspoon baking powder
- 175g/6oz butter or margarine
- 175g/6oz castor sugar
- 3 eggs, beaten until foamy
- 1 tablespoon caraway seeds

# Gingerbread

Grease and line the base of a 20cm/8 inch cake tin. Using a large saucepan warm together the butter or margarine, treacle and syrup. Add the milk and allow to cool. Blend the eggs with the cooled mixture. Sieve the dry ingredients into a bowl, add the cooled mixture and blend with a tablespoon.

Turn into the prepared tin. Bake at 150°C/300°F/gas 2 for $1\frac{1}{4}$–$1\frac{1}{2}$ hours. Turn out and cool on a wire rack.

- 100g/4oz butter or margarine
- 175g/6oz black treacle
- 50g/2oz golden syrup
- 150ml/$\frac{1}{4}$ pint milk
- 2 eggs, beaten
- 225g/8oz flour
- 50g/2oz sugar
- 1 teaspoon mixed spice
- 1 tablespoon ground ginger
- 1 teaspoon bicarbonate of soda

# Christmas Cake

100g/4oz flour
$\frac{1}{2}$ teaspoon mixed spice
100g/4oz butter
100g/4oz soft brown sugar
2 eggs
25g/1oz ground almonds
2 teaspoons grated lemon rind
450g/1lb mixed dried fruit (currants, sultanas, raisins)
25g/1oz chopped nuts (Brazil nuts, walnuts, almonds)
50g/2oz glacé cherries, quartered
50g/2oz mixed peel
apricot jam

*Almond Paste*
225g/8oz ground almonds
225g/8oz icing sugar
1 tablespoon lemon juice
few drops almond essence
2 egg yolks

*Royal Icing*
2 egg whites
450g/1lb icing sugar
$\frac{1}{2}$ teaspoon lemon juice
$\frac{1}{2}$ teaspoon glycerine (optional)

Line the sides and base of an 18cm/7 inch cake tin with a double thickness of greased greaseproof paper. Sift together the flour and mixed spice. Cream the butter and sugar until light and creamy. Beat in the eggs one at a time, adding a tablespoon of the flour with each. Fold in the remaining flour with the ground almonds and lemon rind. Mix in the dried fruit, chopped nuts, cherries and mixed peel.

Spoon into the prepared tin, smooth the surface and make a hollow about 2.5cm/1 inch deep, in the centre. Bake at 150°C/300°F/gas 2 for about $2\frac{1}{2}$ to 3 hours. Cover the top of the cake with greaseproof paper half-way through cooking if it is becoming too brown. When ready, the cake should have slightly drawn away from the sides of the tin; it should spring back when lightly pressed with fingers in the centre; and a skewer pushed into the centre should come out clean.

Leave the cake in the tin to cool slightly, then turn out on to a wire rack and peel off the paper. When quite cold wrap well in greaseproof paper or foil and store in an airtight container for at least a week before putting on the almond paste.

To make the almond paste, mix the ground almonds and icing sugar. Add lemon juice, almond essence and enough egg yolk to form a pliable paste. Knead lightly until smooth and free of cracks. Brush top and sides of the cake with melted and sieved apricot jam. Roll out the paste and cover the top and sides of the cake neatly. Place the cake on a board and leave in a cool, dry place for about 3 days to allow the paste to become dry and firm before icing.

To make the icing, lightly whisk the egg whites. Then gradually sieve in the icing sugar, beating well between each addition, until icing is smooth and stands in stiff peaks. Beat in the lemon juice and glycerine, if used. Ice the top and sides of the cake, either swirling the icing to give a rough finish or smoothing it with a palette knife. Leave to set. Decorate with piped royal icing, if wished. Use a little icing to fix on any bought decorations.

# Madeira Cake

225g/8oz flour
$\frac{1}{2}$ teaspoon baking powder
$\frac{1}{2}$ teaspoon salt
grated rind 1 lemon
175g/6oz butter
175g/6oz castor sugar
4 eggs, beaten
1 tablespoon milk
(optional)
2 or 3 slices citron peel

Grease and flour a 20cm/8 inch cake tin. Sift together the flour, baking powder and salt. Add the lemon rind. Cream together the butter and sugar, beat in the eggs a little at a time. Towards the end of the egg addition, fold in the flour gradually, using a metal tablespoon. Add the milk, if necessary, to give a dropping consistency.

Turn the mixture into the prepared tin and bake at 180°C/350°F/gas 4 for $1\frac{1}{2}$ hours. When the top of the cake is almost set, place the citron peel slices in the centre and finish baking. Turn out and cool on a wire rack.

# Simnel Cake

225g/8oz self-raising flour
1 teaspoon baking powder
1 teaspoon mixed spice
150g/5oz margarine, softened
150g/5oz castor sugar
3 eggs, beaten
½ teaspoon almond essence
75g/3oz mixed peel
175g/6oz currants
175g/6oz sultanas
grated rind 1 lemon
1 tablespoon apricot jam
egg white for glazing

*Almond Paste*
175g/6oz icing sugar
175g/6oz castor sugar
175g/6oz ground almonds
1 large egg, beaten
½ teaspoon vanilla essence

Grease and line an 18cm/7 inch cake tin. Sift the flour, baking powder and mixed spice into a large bowl. Cut the margarine into small pieces and add to the flour with the sugar, eggs and almond essence. Beat until smooth, about 3 minutes by hand or 1 minute with an electric mixer. Stir in the mixed peel, currants, sultanas and grated lemon rind.

To make the almond paste, mix together the sugars and ground almonds. Add the egg and vanilla essence and form into a pliable paste. Knead lightly until smooth and free of cracks.

Cut off one third of the almond paste and roll it into a circle 18cm/7 inches in diameter. Place half the cake mixture in the prepared tin. Level the mixture with a wide spatula and place the circle of almond paste on top. Cover with the remaining cake mixture and level the surface again. Bake at 170°C/325°F/ gas 3 for 2 hours. Leave the cake in the tin to cool slightly before turning it out on to a wire rack.

When the cake is quite cold, brush the top with warmed apricot jam. Roll half the remaining almond paste into a circle 18cm/7 inches in diameter and put on top of the cake. Pinch the edge of the paste to give a decorative finish. Shape the remaining paste into 11 balls (to represent the disciples minus Judas) and put them round the edge of the cake.

Brush the top of the cake and the almond balls with egg white. Brown the cake lightly under a hot grill. Originally the traditional cake for Mothering Sunday, this is nowadays associated with Eastertide.

*Opposite: Summer pudding (recipe page 86).*
*Overleaf: Cheese scones, savoury girdle scones (recipes pages 93, 94).*

GALE'S
HONEY

MUSTARD

227 g 100% PURE
PURE COUNTRY

PICCALILLI
PICCALILLI

# Custard Tarts

*12 tartlets*

Roll out the pastry thinly and use to line 12 tartlet tins. Lightly beat together the eggs and sugar. Heat the milk, but do not bring to boiling point. Pour the hot milk over the beaten eggs, stirring constantly. Allow to cool and strain the mixture into a jug. Pour the custard mixture into the lined tartlet tins and sprinkle each tart with a little nutmeg. Bake at 200°C/400°F/gas 6 for about 20 minutes until the custard has set and the pastry is cooked. Cool on a wire rack.

shortcrust pastry, using 175g/6oz flour etc (see page 15)
2 eggs
25g/1oz castor sugar
250ml/8fl oz milk
grated nutmeg

# Maids of Honour

*12 tartlets*

Roll out the pastry thinly and use to line 12 tartlet tins. Mix the ground almonds and sugar if used. Add the egg and stir in the flour. Add honey if used, and cream or top of the milk. Divide the mixture between the lined tins. Bake at 200°C/400°F/gas 6 for about 25 minutes until set and golden brown. Cool on a wire rack. Dredge with castor or icing sugar.

shortcrust pastry, using 175g/6oz flour etc (see page 15)
100g/4oz ground almonds
50g/2oz castor sugar or 3 tablespoons honey
1 egg, beaten
1 tablespoon flour
2 teaspoons cream or top of the milk
castor or icing sugar

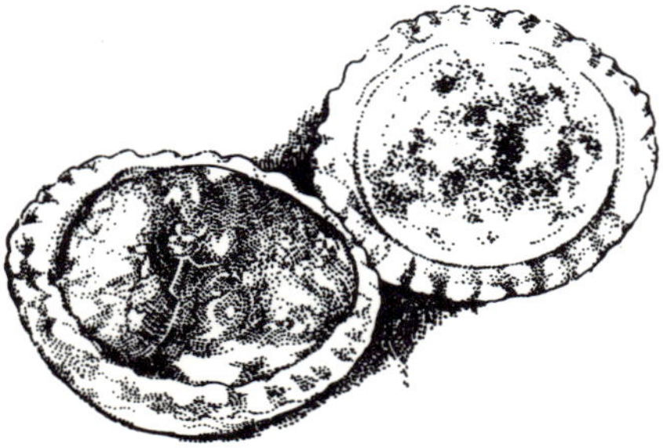

*Previous page: Maids of honour (recipe above).*
*Opposite: Piccalilli (recipe page 107).*

# Brandy Snaps

*20 brandy snaps*

50g/2oz butter
$2\frac{1}{2}$ tablespoons honey or golden syrup
50g/2oz soft brown sugar
50g/2oz flour
$\frac{1}{2}$ teaspoon ground ginger
1 teaspoon brandy or lemon juice
300ml/$\frac{1}{2}$ pint double cream (optional)

Melt the butter, honey or syrup and sugar in a double saucepan or in a heavy pan over a very low heat. Remove from the heat and stir in the remaining ingredients. Place spoonfuls of the mixture 5cm/2 inches apart on well greased baking sheets. Bake at 190°C/375°F/gas 5 for about 4 minutes. Allow to cool slightly before lifting the snaps off the baking sheets one at a time using a palette knife. Roll each snap around the greased handle of a wooden spoon. Slip each rolled snap off the handle as it becomes firm. The brandy snaps may be filled with whipped cream when cold.

# Flapjacks

*24 flapjacks*

100g/4oz butter
3 tablespoons golden syrup
75g/3oz soft brown sugar
225g/8oz rolled oats

Melt the butter, syrup and sugar in a double saucepan or in a heavy pan over a very low heat. Remove from the heat and stir in the rolled oats. Spread the mixture over a greased Swiss roll tin 20 × 30cm/8 × 12 inches. Bake at 180°C/350°F/gas 4 for 25 to 30 minutes, until golden. Leave to stand for a few minutes after baking, then mark into slices. Remove from the tin when cold. Store in an airtight container.

# Pickles & Preserves

## Piccalilli

Prepare the vegetables and chop the marrow, cucumber and green beans into small pieces. Mix the vegetables with the salt in a large bowl. Cover and leave to stand. Put the vinegar into a bowl with the peppercorns, allspice, garlic, root ginger and chilli if used. Stand the bowl in a pan of water, bring the water to the boil, then remove from the heat and cover. Leave the salted vegetables and the spiced vinegar for 24 hours.

Rinse the vegetables well, then drain. Strain the spiced vinegar and reserve 5 tablespoons. Put the remaining vinegar into a saucepan, add the sugar, mustard, turmeric and ground ginger if used. Bring to the boil, stirring. Add the vegetables and simmer for 4 minutes. Blend the cornflour with the reserved vinegar and add to the pan. Simmer for 3 minutes, stirring carefully. Put into warm jars and seal.

450g/1lb marrow
450g/1lb cucumber
450g/1lb green beans
450g/1lb pickling onions
1kg/2lb cauliflower florets
150g/5oz cooking salt

*Dressing*
1.2 litres/2 pints white malt vinegar
15g/½oz black peppercorns
15g/½oz allspice berries
2 cloves garlic, crushed
15g/½oz root ginger, bruised or 2 tablespoons ground ginger
1 chilli pepper (optional)
175g/6oz sugar
2 tablespoons dry mustard
1 tablespoon turmeric
20g/¾oz cornflour

# Carrot and Cucumber Pickle

450g/1lb cucumber
$1\frac{1}{2}$ tablespoons salt
400g/14oz carrots
400ml/$\frac{3}{4}$ pint white malt vinegar
175g/6oz sugar
1 teaspoon dry mustard
$\frac{1}{2}$ teaspoon turmeric

Cut the cucumber into sticks about 5cm × 5mm/ 2 × $\frac{1}{4}$ inch. Place half the cucumber sticks in a bowl, sprinkle with half the salt, add the remaining cucumber and sprinkle with the remaining salt. Cover and leave for 24 hours. Rinse well and drain.

Cut the carrots into sticks the same size as the cucumber. Place in boiling salted water and boil for 2 minutes. Drain well. Put the vinegar, sugar, mustard and turmeric in a pan and bring to the boil. Add the drained cucumber and carrot and simmer for 4 minutes. Pack the vegetable sticks into warm jars and pour over enough hot vinegar to cover. Seal.

# Pickled Red Cabbage

1kg/2lb red cabbage, trimmed and shredded
1 tablespoon salt
600ml/1 pint malt vinegar
25g/1oz pickling spice

Sprinkle the cabbage with salt and set aside in a cool place for 24 hours. Drain well.

Bring the vinegar and pickling spice to the boil, simmer for 5 minutes, strain and set aside. Put the salted cabbage into jars, top up with spiced vinegar and seal.

*Note:* Pickled cabbage is not for long keeping. It may be eaten after 1 week, or stored for up to 2 months.

# Apple Chutney

Put the vinegar, sugar, ginger, mustard and lemon rind and juice into a heavy pan. Bring to the boil. Add the apples, onions and sultanas, and simmer for about 1 hour until the chutney thickens, stirring occasionally to prevent sticking. Allow to cool a little, put into warm jars and seal.

900ml/$1\frac{1}{2}$ pints malt vinegar
1kg/2lb soft brown sugar
2 teaspoons ground ginger
2 teaspoons dry mustard
grated rind and juice 1 lemon
2kg/4lb cooking apples, peeled, cored and chopped
225g/8oz onions, chopped
450g/1lb sultanas

# Mixed Fruit Chutney

Put the vinegar, sugar, spices and orange rind and juice into a heavy pan. Bring to the boil. Add the apples, pears and bananas, and simmer for about 1 hour until thick, stirring occasionally. Allow to cool a little, put into warm jars and seal.

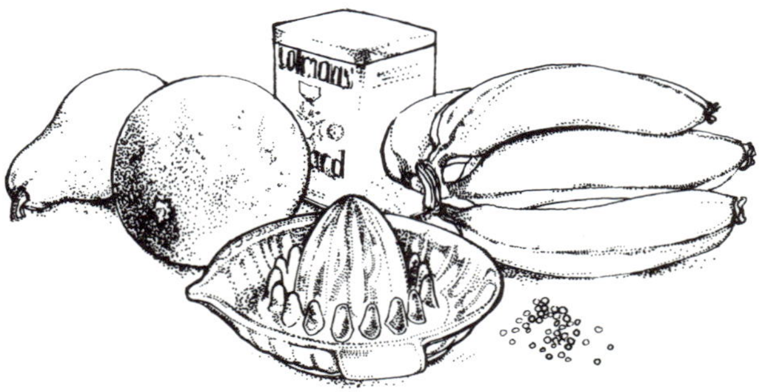

300ml/$\frac{1}{2}$ pint white malt vinegar
750g/$1\frac{1}{2}$lb soft brown sugar
1 teaspoon ground ginger
1 teaspoon dry mustard
1 teaspoon ground cloves
1 teaspoon ground allspice
grated rind and juice 3 oranges
750g/$1\frac{1}{2}$lb cooking apples, peeled, cored and chopped
450g/1lb pears, peeled, cored and chopped
2 bananas, sliced

# Tomato Chutney

400ml/$\frac{3}{4}$ pint malt vinegar
350g/12oz soft brown sugar
15g/$\frac{1}{2}$oz salt
$\frac{1}{2}$ teaspoon ground ginger
2 teaspoons dry mustard
1kg/2lb tomatoes, peeled and chopped
750g/1$\frac{1}{2}$lb cooking apples, peeled, cored and chopped
400g/14oz onions, chopped
350g/12oz sultanas

Put the vinegar, sugar, salt, ginger and mustard into a heavy pan. Bring to the boil. Add the tomatoes, apples, onions and sultanas and simmer for about 1 hour until thick, stirring occasionally. Allow to cool a little, put into warm jars and seal.

# Lemon Curd

50g/2oz butter
175g/6oz sugar
grated rind and juice 1 large lemon
1 egg
3 egg yolks

Melt the butter and sugar with the lemon rind and juice in a heavy saucepan or the inner pan of a double boiler. Beat up the egg and egg yolks and add to the other ingredients. Heat gently until the mixture thickens, stirring frequently. Pour into warm jars. Cover when cold. Use as a scone spread or as a tartlet filling.

# Index